GUIDO CAVALCANTI

THE COMPLETE POEMS

GUIDO CAVALCANTI

THE COMPLETE POEMS

TRANSLATED WITH AN INTRODUCTION
AND NOTES BY
MARC A. CIRIGLIANO

ITALICA PRESS
NEW YORK
1992

ITALICA PRESS, INC.
595 Main Street
New York, New York 10044

Library of Congress Cataloging-in-Publication Data

Cavalcanti, Guido. d. 1300.
    [Works. English & Italian. 1992]
    The complete poems / Guido Cavalcanti ; translated with an
introduction and notes by Marc A. Cirigliano.
       p. cm.
    English and Italian.
    Includes bibliographical references and index.
    ISBN 0-934977-27-5 : $10.00
    1. Cavalcanti, Guido, d. 1300--Translations into English.
I. Cirigliano. Marc A., 1952- . II. Title.
PQ4299.C2 1992
851' .1--dc20   92-12123
                                                     CIP

Printed in the United States of America
5 4 3 2

Cover illustration: "Donna me prega" from Cornell Univ., Petrarch MSS Bd P.P49.R51, fol. 132v
Courtesy of Cornell University Library, Department of Rare Books

For Lindy,
Dan and Matt

About the Translator

A Florence Fellow and Ph.D. from Syracuse University, Marc Cirigliano teaches interdisciplinary fine arts at a college in upstate New York. His interests include the Italian Renaissance, nineteenth-century Romanticism, and aesthetics. He is presently finishing a contemporary poetic translation of Dante's complete lyric poetry and working on an interdisciplinary book on creativity, entitled *Some Unseen Power.*

CONTENTS

ACKNOWLEDGEMENTS

I could think of no single group that would be more responsible for my ability to bring this creative and scholarly project to fruition than many of my former teachers at Syracuse University. Sidney Thomas, Anna Maria Moneti, Catherine Lord, and Meredith Lillich taught me to read with insight, sensitivity, and curiosity in a wide variety of areas. John Clarke Adams taught me to love the past and what is beautiful in the world. His insistence that Sibilla Aleramo made more sense than Descartes when she wrote "I love, therefore I am" has not been taken lightly. The late Luisa Becherucci and the late Ugo Procacci, both wonderful teachers, taught me that philological exactitude without aesthetic sensitivity is meaningless.

My friends Karen Martin Tomaselli and Tony "Il Massimo" Favro provided me with countless hours of insightful discussion about creativity. Three colleagues at Empire State College/SUNY gave me tremendous encouragement at the inception of this project: George Drury, Robert Milton, and Robert Seidel. Finally, my editors and publishers at Italica Press, Eileen Gardiner and Ron Musto, were more than helpful.

INTRODUCTION

This translation of the poems of Guido Cavalcanti is intended for people who love to read.[1] I hope to make Cavalcanti accessible for an English-reading audience. A particular hope is that readers take my translation with Robert Haas' advice, "It is listening that I am interested in – in writers and readers – and the kind of making [of poetry] that can come from live, attentive listening."[2] There is, alternatively, a danger that such reading might possibly lead to over-intellectualizing Cavalcanti's poetry to the point that it, like any utterance in a tavern, becomes merely a socially produced text for critical dissection. So I ask that the reader remember that this translation was done with that dictum of Benedetto Croce always in the back of the translator's mind: "The understanding of poetry goes straight to that poetic heart and feels it beat within his own; and where that beating stops, he denies that it is poetry...."[3]

The following essay serves as a simple introduction to the experiences of Cavalcanti as a human being, as a creative artist, and as a thinker delving into the human condition. His was a realm of deep feelings and incessant questioning about the broad spectrum of human relationships and their potentialities.

The Man and His Times

Guido Cavalcanti (c.1250-1300) was, next to Dante Alighieri, the best poet of the early Italian Renaissance. These two Florentines were the prime movers behind a new type of love poetry developed in Florence in the second half of the thirteenth century known as the *dolce stil nuovo* (literally, the "Sweet New Style"). Other, less important, poets in the movement were Lapo Gianni, Gianni Alfani, Dino Frescobaldi, and Cino da Pistoia. The *dolce stil nuovo* was a fresh approach to the tradition of medieval love poetry begun in Provence in the twelfth century by the male troubadours and female trobairitzes. The troubadours invented a brilliant poetic style that narrated the sequences of the events and personal feelings involved in polite, or courtly, love. The *stilnovisti,* particularly Dante and Guido with their expansive intellectual sensitivity, took this basic formula and developed it into a philosophical inquiry about love itself.

Cavalcanti lived an active political, literary, and personal life among the turbulence of early Renaissance Florence.[4] There is scant information on Cavalcanti's youth and education, but the existing historical documentation reveals a man with a strong personality, afraid of neither political nor artistic challenges.

He was born to a wealthy, distinguished, and politically active Florentine family, the son of Cavalcante Cavalcanti. Along with that of his younger colleague Dante, Guido's early education was influenced by Brunetto Latini, who placed a particular emphasis on the role of rhetoric and classical literature. It would seem plausible to draw parallels between Cavalcanti's education and what we know to be Dante's. Early on in grammar school, Dante studied Cato from the *Disticha Catonis,* Aesop from the *Liber Esopi,* and the Bible. He also received basic instruction in grammar and arithmetic, the contemporary essentials for life in a commercial center like Florence. In adolescence, he also read from Boethius' *De consolatione philosophiae* (the Consolation of Philosophy); Cicero's *De amicitia* (On Friendship), *De officiis* (On Duties), and *De senectute* (On Old Age); and the works of Aristotle. Cavalcanti was also intimately familiar with, and strongly influenced by, the works of Averroës, the Islamic philosopher and commentator on Aristotle. Like most aristocratic youth of his day,

Cavalcanti received basic training in the military skills required of his class and urban citizenship.

Like Dante, Cavalcanti seems to have been familiar with many Provençal, Sicilian, and classical poets. Of the latter, Dante speaks of Homer (known in Latin translation), Horace, Lucan, Ovid, and Virgil. We also know that Dante studied the *Elegia* of the twelfth-century Italian poet, Arrigo da Settimello. In the intellectual climate of Florence, no small influence would have been the Franciscan mysticism centered at the convent of Santa Croce and the influence of the Dominican Thomas Aquinas at Santa Maria Novella.[5]

At mid-thirteenth century, Florence, an independent commune or city-state, was divided into two political factions, the Guelph party, mostly allied with the pope, and the Ghibelline party, often allied with the Holy Roman emperor. In 1260, the Ghibellines gained ascendancy in Florence by defeating the Guelphs at the battle of Montaperti. In 1266 at Benevento, the Guelphs routed the Ghibellines, who were forever banished from Florence. At this time, Cavalcanti's family began to play a major role in Florentine politics. By the end of the century, the Guelphs split into two factions: the White Guelphs who allied themselves with Ghibelline parties in Verona, Pisa, and the Romagna; and the Black Guelphs who favored the expansionist-minded papacy of Boniface VIII. The Whites were led by the nouveau riche Vieri de' Cerchi, the Blacks by the self-satisfied patrician Corso Donati.

As a young man, Cavalcanti refused to become a member of one of the guilds or to participate in public office, although, along with other members of his family, he supported the Guelf party. His refusal to hold public office may have been due to an attempted reconciliation between the White and Black factions, as part of which he married Bice degli Uberti, the daughter of the head of the Black faction. They had one son, Andrea, who died after 1340. Guido's position in the Florentine aristocracy afforded him the opportunity to serve with Brunetto Latini as one of the guarantors of Cardinal Latino's peace treaty in 1280. Although the documentation is inconclusive, in 1284 he might have been spurred to become a member of Florence's city council or the podestà as the result of renewed political strife in Florence.

Soon after, he was a supporter of the White Guelf faction and a dire enemy of Corso Donati in a communal conflict that had a bloody history. Corso tried to have Guido assassinated in Galizia when the young Cavalcanti was on a pilgrimage to Santiago de Compostela in Spain. On a later occasion, in 1292, Guido was out riding when he came across Corso. Cavalcanti charged, throwing a hunting spear at Corso. Unfortunately, he missed. Corso and his party gave chase. Although they did not catch him, they threw stones at Guido, wounding him in the hand.

On December 16, 1297, he took part in the assault on the house of the Donati. Later, he was involved in inciting the Cerchi family to attack the Donati in the Donati's own neighborhood. For this last action, he received a heavy fine from the city. The political acrimony did not stop there. In 1300, Dante, as a member of the six-member Priory, or ruling government of Florence, was forced into what had to be one of the most difficult decisions of his life. He would do what he felt to be the right thing while trying to preserve the independence of Florence. On May Day, the Donati and Cerchi families were watching the festive dancing. An armed fight broke out between the families. Dante and his fellow Priors exiled the heads of both factions. Guido Cavalcanti, Dante's best friend, was sent to Sarzana. Guido became ill, perhaps with malaria, and was allowed to return to Florence, where he died in August and, as the historian Filippo Villani relates in his *Lives of*

Illustrious Florentines, "was buried among the tears of the good citizens."

Contemporary portraits of Cavalcanti reveal a man of great passion with tremendous artistic and intellectual abilities. In his *Chronicle,* Dino Compagni described Guido as "courteous and daring, but disdainful, solitary, and devoted to study." Fillipo Villani wrote that he "was a virtuous philosopher in many things, although too sensitive and hotheaded." In his *Commentary* on Dante's *Divine Comedy* Boccaccio described Cavalcanti as "well educated, rich, of high intelligence, and more knowledgeable and able than any of our citizens in many things. At the same time, he was a good philosopher and the best logician." In the *Decameron,* Boccaccio echoes this praise, reinforcing the notion that Guido was "one of the best logicians in the world and the best natural philosopher." Giorgio Petrocchi, the twentieth-century Italian critic, emphasizes that not unimportant in understanding Guido's poetic originality was Dante's depiction of him in Canto X of the *Inferno* as a "free spirit and nonconformist, capable of detaching himself from the general tendencies of his environment and epoch."[6]

The Poetry of Courtly Love

The poetry of courtly love was born in the aristocratic courts of Provence in the south of France, in the early twelfth century, where a new concept of sincere love, or *fin'amors,* was developed. Their achievements were emulated by the poets in the Sicilian court of Frederick II. The Florentine *stilnovisti* drew from both schools of poetry in developing their *dolce stil nuovo.*[7] Even though their inspiration came from foreign courts, the actual poem that served as the prototype for them was written by Guido Guinizelli, a Bolognese poet who lived in the second half of the thirteenth century.[8] His poem "Al cor gentil repara sempre Amore" summarizes the major idea developed in the poetry of courtly love: "Love always seeks the gently virtuous heart."[9]

This genteel concept springs directly from the concept of chivalry, which embodied an ideal of behavior stressing that knights should leave their lion-hearted fierceness on the battlefield and bring only gentleness and refinement into the aristocratic household of the court. Refined manners became the mark of good breeding. The key element in this refined behavior at court was the emphasis on the overt relations between nobles and ladies. If a nobleman in any way acted crudely in the face of the court – either with force or rude manners – he was discredited and considered unworthy of his high position, let alone given any chance to play at love. If he had worth and acted with gentle virtue toward ladies, they might show mercy or pity by favoring him with their love. A lady's love might be merely a glance of approval. However, it also could take either the form of Christian *caritas* in becoming an on-going intellectual conversation with the lady, or it could become earthly love by leading to a covert relationship reveling in sexual intimacy.[10]

Such songs of poetically refined passion were probably the major reason that the level of cultural attainment of the courts of Provence was so admired by the Italians to the south.[11] However, there was one major difference between the Florentine *stilnovisti* and the French troubadours. While the French celebrated love among the select at court, the Florentines philosophized about it in a blossoming urban environment.[12] And by philosophizing about it, the implications and ramifications of love as a process were explored.

Importance of Allegory

The poetry of the *stilnovisti* narrates the moment the two lovers' eyes meet, discusses the feeling and motives of the Lady and her beloved, and explicitly and implicitly investigates the essence of physical and spiritual love. It consists of multiple levels of meaning. It is, then, allegorical. Allegory was common in much of the literature and art of Cavalcanti's epoch. Allegory compares two different things and points out a parallelism between the two or even a structural relationship that ties them together. For example, the numbers that one used to keep the books in a leather business in Florence were thought to be the very essence of God's design of the cosmos. Consequently, numbers served as the basis for Renaissance church design.[13]

A similar analogy could be drawn for Renaissance views of history and poetry. Poetry was similar to history in that it narrated the events of past human activity. It was different from history in that it did not present occurrences as they happened, but instead, embellished them. History was grounded in truth, poetry in a reasonable imitation of that truth. However, poetry and history served the same end because both taught proper moral action. Since poetry did not teach events as they happened, but related them by means of metaphor and analogy, these very same analogies and metaphors ran parallel to the historical truth. To decipher them was one way to discover the truth. Dante reasoned that after establishing a literal meaning, the allegorical one could be ascertained in order to more fully understand the truth:

> And so, since the establishment of meaning is something constructed by systematic study, and since the establishment of the literal meaning is the foundation of the other meanings, particularly the allegorical, it is impossible to arrive at the others before the literal.
>
> Furthermore, even were it possible, it would be irrational, that is, out of proper order, and therefore a tiring and erratic process. For, as the Philosopher says in the first book of the *Physics*, Nature wishes our procedure of discovery to be orderly, proceeding

from what we know well to what we know not so well.[14]

We can see, then, that the use and study of allegory was considered one of the systematic ways to study.[15]

The same type of analogy provided for contemporary cross-references between academic disciplines. For example, love was considered a gift from God, a grace if you will, that was a shadow of His own love for all humanity. To be God or Christ-like, then, was to love fellow men and women in a certain way. In this sense, theology and politics mutually enlighten one another. Other analogies were possible. Love was also a type of activity that embodied parallel goals in different categories of endeavor. Haller explains:

> Ladies and disciplines, for instance, may both be pursued; they may both attract a man with the promise of granting happiness; they may both at times put difficulties in the way of their pursuers; but they will both reward a persistent effort by granting knowledge of the inner sources of their attractive appearances. A noble lady is thus an appropriate figure for the noble disciplines of philosophy, and, through the comparison, the purposes of human love may be manifested.[16]

Hence, allegory, with its multiple meanings, lends itself to the fuller comprehension of the truth. Moreover, if we accept C. S. Lewis's contention that medieval allegory was used to "explore the inner world" of the human mind in an age that did not know about "personality" in our modern sense, then our need to comprehend Cavalcanti's specific poetic imagery becomes all the more compelling.[17]

Woman as Ideal

Using the allegorical concept of multiple levels of meaning, the *stilnovisti* created images of ideal women who served as allegories for numerous human interests: the pursuit of knowledge, artistic creation, humanity's relationship to God, male-female, social, personal, political, and diplomatic relations, intellectual debate, and of course, matters of truth and virtue. The underlying assumption of all these activities is the desire for harmony between two different entities, be they the student and a subject, a beloved and his lady, or a head of state and an emissary. Given the political and personal strife ever-present in Florence during this time, it is not surprising that love and the conditions necessary for it are being investigated. In times of famine, people are usually concerned about food.

One of the central points about this new viewpoint concerns the "ideal" and the suitor. The man must now watch how he acts. No matter what the lady symbolizes in the poetry, in reality she has become a human being worthy of deference.[18] In a word, the man must become civilized. The early twentieth-century philosopher, José Ortega y Gasset, explains the two-pronged assumption of such a process. First, one must take others into consideration:

> Restrictions, standards, courtesy, indirect methods, justice, reason! Why were all these invented, why all these complications created? They are all summed up in the word civilization, which, through the underlying notion of *civis*, the citizen, reveals its real origin. By means of all these there is an attempt to make possible the city, the community, common life. Hence, if we look into all these constituents of civilization just enumerated, we shall find the same common basis. All, in fact, presuppose the radical progressive desire on the part

of each individual to take others into considera-
tion. Civilization is before all, the will to live in
common. A man is uncivilized, barbarian in the
degree in which he does not take others into
account.[19]

Second, the concept of civilization presupposes that
people should transcend their own immediate subjectivity
and gratification. They should recognize a standard
beyond their own narrow drives and desires. Ortega ob-
served:

...the select man, the excellent man is urged, by
interior necessity, to appeal from himself to some
standard beyond himself, superior to himself,
whose service he freely accepts....This life is lived as
a discipline – the noble life. Nobility is defined by
the demands it makes on us – by obligations, not
rights. Noblesse oblige. "To live as one likes is
plebeian: the noble man aspires to order and law"
(Goethe).[20]

This two-fold process is at the root of the *stilnovisti's*
poetry. One must recognize other individuals and stan-
dards beyond oneself. Cavalcanti and Dante, even more
than the other *stilnovisti*, poeticize this process using an
ideal.[21] In *De Vulgari Eloquentia,* Dante affirms this quest
for excellence, the appeal to a standard beyond the mere
individual:

For, insofar as we act simply as human beings, we
have virtue (as understood in its general sense),
according to which we judge a man good or bad;
insofar as we act as human beings who are citizens,
we have the law, according to which we judge a
good or bad citizen; insofar as we act as Italians, we
have certain very simple standards of customs and
manners and speech, by which our actions as
Italians are weighed and measured.[22]

In *De Monarchia,* he describes the faculties of the human intellect as "all alike handmaids of speculation, as the supreme function for which the Prime Excellence brought the human race into being."[23] In sum, the principles of human behavior and human artistic creation are underscored by a principle of excellence that serves to ennoble humanity.[24] Cavalcanti echoes this recognition of an standard beyond himself when, in concluding his *ballata* "Era in penser d'amor," he commands it to:

> *Vanne a Tolosa, ballatetta mia,*
> *ed entra quetamente a la Dorata,*
> *ed ivi chiama che per cortesia*
> *d'alcuna bella donna sie menata*
> *dinanzi a quella di cui t'ho pregata;*
> *e s'ella ti riceve,*
> *dille con voce leve:*
> *"Per merzé vegno a voi."*

> go to Tolosa, my ballatetta,
> and enter Notre-Dame de la Daurade
> and ask if by courtesy
> a particular beautiful Lady is there
> it's before her i ask you to go
> and if she receives you
> tell her out loud –
> i come to you for Mercy.[25]

It is clear that in entering the process of love, Cavalcanti is accepting an authority outside himself, an authority that is refined and civil. In the face of the free will of his intended, he assiduously regulates his own behavior, hoping for a more profound end than mere sexual satisfaction.

It is at this point that we can begin to see the individual quality that makes Cavalcanti's work different from that of the other *stilnovisti.* His emphasis on the irreconcilability of human relationships – literally his own or allegorically those of a social, political, or religious nature – indicates what must have been a profound sense of alienation. For all the civility overtly present, Cavalcanti expresses a strong inner dissatisfaction and anger with relationships that he finds incomplete. Such anger, much in the same way as fear from an individual threatened by physical violence, demands only one question: Why?

In short, Guido is looking deeply into the human psyche for the cause of strife in human relationships. Yet he renders his findings in a manner that conveys serious intellectual content with the most profound and sincere pathos and empathy. There is a contemporary urgency in this verse, not to understand sex, but to come to grips with the impelling nature of human *passion,* that motivating force behind all human strife, be it personal, social, or political. His *rime* were not simply cries in the wilderness, but poignant public utterances meant to stimulate the issue. Mario Marti explains that "the new poetics did not blossom weakly in closed circles, but descended to the streets, totally laid bare, ready to sustain encounters and clashes that would leave their mark." Because of his depth of feeling and poetic intensity, Cavalcanti stands at the forefront of this movement that "takes us back to the bitter measures, the sense and color of a militant culture against the background of the life and history of the Commune [of Florence]."[26]

Cavalcanti's Pessimism

Cavalcanti and Dante arrived at different conclusions regarding the quest for the ideal posed by the question of love. Both were influenced by different strains of contemporary philosophy. Not simply content to regurgitate the philosophy he encountered, Cavalcanti used it productively to expand his thought so that he might explain the "Why?" of the actual world.

Dante, inspired by the theology of St. Thomas Aquinas, concluded that one must deny the physical body in the quest for love and truth. In his *Vita Nuova*, Beatrice dies and ascends to heaven. The love she and Dante share can never become lust. Instead, it becomes a completely spiritual quest. The purity of their physical bodies is maintained according to the tenets of their faith, and their individual souls are saved.

Cavalcanti rejected Thomistic Christianity for the ideas of Averroës, the twelfth-century Islamic philosopher who commented at length upon the writings of Aristotle.[27] Averroës maintained the Aristotelian tradition of conceiving the human as a being with three basic capacities. The first was a vegetative life, in which the human held certain similarities to plants. The second was a sensitive life that the human shared with animals. The third was an intellectual capacity that distinguished humanity from the first two lower forms of life. According to Averroës, the life proper to humanity was the cultivation of the intellect according to reason, a distinctly human ability.

The crucial point that makes Guido specifically an Averroist and not simply a Thomistic Aristotelian is that Averroës maintained that the intellectual part of a human being was part of a universal consciousness that all intellects came from and eventually returned to after death. This meant two things. First, there was no afterlife. Second, one's intellectual faculties had no individual identity per se. The faculty that gave a person his or her individual identity was the sensitive faculty – one's body. The goal for an Averroist, then, was the perfection of this sensitive faculty by means of the reason of the intellect. This rational end, if brought to the ultimate balance and harmony within an individual, was considered the *buon perfetto* or *bonum perfectum* by the thinkers of Cavalcanti's epoch. The final cause or goal of human life, then, was reasoning that resulted in a balance between the body's physical desires and the intellect.

Cavalcanti considered love a passion that prevented the *buon perfetto* from ever being achieved by an individual. He saw love as a passion innate in humanity. It was a feeling not opposed to nature, but part and parcel of a natural desire. This clearly demonstrates his debt to the troubadours. However, Guido made love less a beneficent emotion than did traditional troubadours. While they viewed love under the benevolent astrological influence of Venus as an ennoblement of erotic passion achieved by means of virtue and beautiful manners, Guido portrayed love as a turbid sentiment malignly influenced by Mars that diminished reason and against which it was useless to rebel. His personification of Love keeps the traditional medieval trappings of a feudal lord with a realm to govern, a servant or retinue of ladies, and, possibly, a bow and arrows, or simply darts.[28] Bruno Nardi clarifies that Guido's Love was not a divinity, but was something created and generated by human activity, a product of the sensitive soul, not the rational intellect.[29]

For Averroës, as well as Aristotle, the one sound way of achieving the *bonum perfectum* was to attain a balance between two extremes of behavior, better known as the "mean." The implications of this scheme for satisfying the urge for love are revelatory. Since love was a natural desire, it asked to be satisfied within the bounds of nature. On the one hand, abstinence was seen as an incessant battle to suppress a wholly natural and constant drive, thereby eliminating any possible serenity necessary for the ultimate felicity of the *buon perfetto*. On the other hand, constant indulgence in this desire was not a satisfactory response, either, as it produced a rashness that was beyond the bounds of "good perfection." The body would come to dominate the intellect.

The specific problem for Guido, and the one that caused the Italian scholar, Bruno Nardi, to label him as a pessimist, was that for Cavalcanti even moderation in satisfying the natural desire of love was impossible. It was not for want of a sound concept of the mean, but for the malign influence that love exercised over the reasoning intellect. In order for love to become satisfied and tamed, the lover and the object of his passion, his beloved, had to be in harmony. This was a state often represented in Guido's poetry as the exchange of *dolci sguardi,* or sweet glances, between two lovers who possessed the lofty intellectual and social virtues that made them worthy of love. The Cavalcantian problem is that this visual inter-action causes a confusion in the lover so that he can neither move forward to complete his task nor can he in any way win his lady. His sensible appetite has overtaken him so that his intellect and judgment are impaired. Hence, we have the "pessimism" that Nardi speaks of. Dante's love ends in an eternal spiritual fulfillment, Guido's in the "death" of reason.

As we shall see in Guido's poems, he dies constantly, only to return to a similar circumstance governed by the same Averroist law that rules the human psyche. Again, however, this is not a simple regurgitation of contem-porary philosophy. His own experience and observation of human relationships leads him to conclude that relation-ships can only lead to one death after another as the sorrowing spirit of the intellect flees one's weeping sen-sitive soul. Guido's position is all the more telling when we realize, as Nardi explains, that in Dante's *Inferno* (X), he is consigned the status of an atheist. While Dante generally sought for a *theological* explanation of the nature of love, Cavalcanti looked for a *natural* or secular one. His pathos is one of the first deep stirrings of an individual inquiry about reality. This is given dramatic artistic form in an individualized expression: the Middle Ages begin to fade as the Florentine Renaissance begins.[30]

Creating a New Language

At this point in time, a new language is created in Florence, that, in large part, becomes the foundation for modern Italian. Although the primary credit for this linguistic innovation rightfully goes to Dante, we should remember that Cavalcanti also played an important role. In the *Vita Nuova* (ch. XXX) Dante writes that "my intention from the beginning was none other than writing in the vernacular." He continues, "I know that my best friend had similar intentions." The best friend was, of course, Guido Cavalcanti.

In *De Vulgari Eloquentia,* Dante gives three reasons for choosing the vernacular over "grammar" or Latin. It was the first type of language used by humanity. It is used by the entire world, but in different pronunciations. His final reason is "because it is natural to us."[31] In fact, the roots of the new vernacular lie in the realm of what is natural as opposed to what Dante termed "artificial." The "illustrious" quality of the vernacular, the *sermo humilis,* the "comic style," the expressive variety of the vernacular, and the borrowing of vocabulary from Provençal all shared a connection with the heartbeat of actual life that people lived. Dante, Cavalcanti and the rest of the *stilnovisti* saw in this simple colloquiality something that made it – to use Dante's phrase from *De Vulgari Eloquentia* – "the more noble."[32]

The simplicity and naturalness of the vernacular was in complete keeping with his description of it as "illustrious." Dante stated that "what we mean by illustrious and why we call it illustrious" is because it is "brilliant, illuminated and illuminating." He makes an analogy with illustrious historic figures because "in this sense we call men illustrious, either because, illuminated by power, they illumine others with justice and charity, or because being excellently ruled they rule excellently, like Numa Pompilius and Seneca." He concludes that "the vernacular with which we are dealing is both exalted by discipline and power and exalts its followers with honor and glory." It is a form of communication that has the discipline to "emerge from so many uncouth Italian words, so many tangled constructions and defective pronunciations, such ugly accents, as a chosen instrument, elegant, clear, complete, polished, as may be seen in the *canzoni* of Cino da Pistoia and his friend [Dante, himself]." Further, it has the power to "change human hearts, making men do what they would not, and refrain from what they would, as this language has done and still does."[33] This newly forming natural vernacular, then, has the power to persuade people by its simple and clear elegance.

Chivalric love gives rise to the first sublime poetic style since antiquity. The poetry of courtly love has both a lofty subject and a lofty form, the two major components of the elevated genre, the *stilus tragicus*.[34] However, in the case of Dante and Cavalcanti, they achieve a lofty sublimity in a very particular way. They follow the medieval practice of using the *sermo humilis*. The *sermo humilis* was a simple, direct, and colloquial Latin style developed by the early Christians that was a deliberate rejection of literary Latin. In following this rhetorical practice, Dante and Cavalcanti set themselves apart even from the Provençal and Sicilian poets, who while writing in their own respective vernaculars, wrote in literary versions of them. Dante and Cavalcanti wrote in their spoken vernacular. This further intensifies one of the strong points of the *sermo humilis* as a rhetorical device that, as Auerbach explains, has the "implication of direct human contact between you and me, a note that was lacking in the sublime style of Roman antiquity."[35]

Communicating the immediacy of feelings was central to the *dolce stil nuovo*. When Dante describes an oxymoronic "illustrious vernacular" in his *De Vulgari Eloquentia*, he makes it plain that he is using a language that has two qualities. It is not removed from the simple practicality of everyday life. It is also capable of expressing lofty ideas. Although he begins *De Vulgari Eloquentia* emphasizing that the vernacular is what "even women and children seek," he is not trying to demean. After all, he would be denigrating his own work. He is emphasizing that he is using the language of those not trained in Latin in order to reach a new audience.

Dante and the *stilnovisti* rejection of the pretensions of literary Latin in favor of something more "natural" signals a new age for European literature. In his famous letter to Can Grande della Scala, Dante expressed openly that while *"alta tragedia"* was in principle admirable, in practice he thought it "fetid and horrible." He preferred, instead, to develop a new poetic idiom, the *"stile comico."* The major aims of the comic style were not humorous but dealt with communicative colloquiality and poetic realism. Schiaffini writes that "the theory of the comic style permits an unbridled variety of use, an authentic polyglotism, including dialects that were foreign to Florentine...." This linguistic variety provided Dante (and, I believe, Cavalcanti) with "a varied tonality with which he...adapted to different states of the soul and different places and times...."[36] Petrocchi explains that this change in Dante's language adds:

> obscure, dense, profound rumblings and rhythms impatiently prolonged, an obscure and harsh voice that will recite words of anguish and restlessness of passion....[37]

To consider Dante and Cavalcanti's language simply a "sweet new style" of their existing vernacular, then, is completely inaccurate. Within this new vernacular, an extreme variety of feeling was expressed. Dante and Cavalcanti looked at all the possibilities of love. The *dolce* (sweetness) of the *dolce stil nuovo* was not by any means its only or even dominant attribute.[38] They also used language that was *aspro* or harsh, the opposite of *dolce*.

These two terms, with their respective smooth and rough sonority, are proper forms for the embodiment of one of the central ideas of this poetry: *dolci tormenti,* or sweet torments. Between these extremes Cavalcanti expresses a variety of natural emotions: joy, sorrow, pleasure, dejection, ecstasy, utter collapse, satisfaction, wonderment, alienation, stupefaction, and many other nuances.

In creating this new vocabulary, the *stilnovisti* borrowed vocabulary from both the Provençal troubadours and the Sicilians court poets.[39] They wanted to evoke a deliberate association with the high literary culture of Provence as well as the court of Frederick II in Sicily. Provençal provided the *stilnovisti* with the gamut of ideas and feelings central to love poetry: *amanza* (lover or sweetheart), *intendanza* (one's intended or betrothed), *gioia* (joy), *alma* (soul), *coraggio* and *corina* (heart), *simblanza* (appearance), *speranza* (hope), *talento* (desire), *rimembranza* (recollection), *gente* (genteel, noble, or cultured), *uccidere* (to kill), *scegliere* (to choose), *esaltare* (to exalt).[40]

The borrowing did not stop here. They also incorporated words from Bolognese, Umbrian, and other Italian dialects into their own native Tuscan and Florentine. A point of key interest is that contemporary Tuscan manuscript copyists, in transcribing the poets of Sicily, maintained some of the original Sicilian vocabulary in order to evoke favorable associations with the culture established at the court of Frederick II. At other times, they gave certain words a "rinse in the Arno" to Tuscanize them.[41] It is fascinating to note that the tradition of love poetry created a nearly common language for poetry in Italy at this time. This development was not carried over to prose, which for the most part remained in local dialect. Migliorini attributes this to the fact that prose was used in strictly local, day-to-day matters, while poetry was regularly communicated among the various regions.[42] Common use fostered common language.

Cavalcanti, then, helps to create this new "illustrious vernacular." He uses it to achieve a fusion of form and content that expresses both the pleasures of love as well as its torments. He, as much as Dante, leaves the soft elegance of the Sicilian school behind, seeking newer, more expressive plateaus. For example, in "Tu m'hai sì piena di dolor la mente," he begins by using sweet-sounding words to tell of his current enamored state:

> *Tu m'hai sì piena di dolor la mente,*
> *che l'anima si briga di partire...*

> you've so filled my mind with pain
> my soul hurries to leave....

Everything in the first line suggests the potential tenderness of love by flowing smoothly until the second line introduces, with its rough edge, the impending failure of this relationship. The poem eventually culminates with the lover dying, his soul fleeing, and death transforming him into solid matter:

> *ch'omo sia*
> *fatto di rame o di pietra o di legno,...*

> a man
> made of bronze or stone or wood....

Here, the hard sound of staccato, *aspro,* consonants stands in sharp contrast to the soft, *dolce,* liquid consonants and vowels of the first line. We should not forget, in reading Cavalcanti, that at times he is capable of the same wide range of expression and bitingly rough edge that Dante will achieve.[43]

Cavalcanti's verse is both similar to, and different from, other *stilnovisti.* For example, the work of Lapo Gianni seems, by comparison, quite tame. His work flows smoothly but does not reveal love to be a gripping event that goes to the center of one's being. In "Dolc'è 'l pensier che mi notrica il core," he writes:

Ella mi fe' tanta di cortesia
che no sdegnò mio soave parlare;
ond'i' voglio Amor dolce ringraziare
che me fe' degno di cotanto onore.

She showed me such courtesy
that she disdained not my words;
so I wanted to thank Love
who made me worthy of such honor.[44]

The poetry is elegant, perhaps even light, but it does not have the poetic force of Cavalcanti's intellectual drama.[45] Lapo does not plead and weep, and his women do not inflict other than contrived cruelty.

This is not to say that Cavalcanti was the greatest lyric poet of his time. That honor, of course, belongs to Dante, whose *Vita Nuova* and *Divine Comedy* are the apotheosis of the *dolce stil nuovo*.

Victorian Cavalcanti?

Cavalcanti's work was previously translated into English by two of our best-known poets: the Pre-Raphaelite Dante Gabriel Rossetti in the nineteenth century and Ezra Pound in the twentieth. Some comments on their versions will prove helpful in understanding both Cavalcanti's language and the present translation.

The biggest mistake that Rossetti made in translating the *stilnovisti* poets was that he used an English that was deliberately archaic to the ears of the nineteenth century. Although this might seem to capture the elegance of the *stilnovisti*, it is, given the historical fact that their language was far more diverse and contemporary than simply elegant, a false and misleading notion. For example, he translates the first stanza of Cavalcanti's "Vedeste, al mio parere," as:

Unto my thinking, thou beheld'st all worth,
All joy, as much of good as man may know,

If thou wert in his power who here below
Is honour's righteous lord throughout this earth.[46]

Words such as "thou," "beheld'st," and "wert" were anti-
quated far earlier than the mid-nineteenth century when
Rossetti was using them to render his version of
Cavalcanti.

This type of old-fashioned vocabulary was something
that Cavalcanti, Dante, and others avoided deliberately by
means of their upbeat, contemporary, and original use of
the varieties of their own and other vernaculars. They
were in the process of inventing a new language, a proce-
dure that was anything but archaic or polite. What could
be more contemporary and intentionally "comical" than
Dante's practice of mixing Italian dialects in order to
arrive at a spelling that fits his rhyme scheme? Schiaffini
points to Dante's creative cheating when he uses the
bastardized Latin *introque* (among us) to rhyme with
nocque (to harm) in the *Inferno* (XX, 128-30). Both Dante
and Cavalcanti use the Bolognese *lome* for the more
familiar *lume* (light) in order to rhyme with *come*.
Further, Dante uses the Umbrian *vonno* instead of *vanno*
(they go) in the *Paradiso* (XXVIII, 101-3) in order to
match *ponno*.[47] When it suits his ear, Cavalcanti even
switches first person pronouns, using the Florentine *io*
and the Sicilian influenced *eo*.[48] In short, the grammat-
ical propriety implied by Rossetti's Victorian pretensions
connotes a Guido that never existed.

Much the same charge can be leveled at Pound, who
also used an antiquated English when he translated
Cavalcanti earlier in this century. But there is a flaw in
his work beyond giving the wrong connotation with
outdated English. His work is replete with inaccurate
translations. Pound explained his primary aim:

> I have in my translations tried to bring over the
> qualities of Guido's rhythm, not line for line, but

to embody in the whole of my English some trace
of that power which implies the man.[49]

There is an ever-present power of rhythm in his
translation. Pound also attempts to match Cavalcanti's
own rhyme schemes. In "Tu m'hai sì piena di dolor la
mente," Pound translates:

> Thou hast my mind so high heaped up with grief,
> That my soul irks him to be on the road,
> Mine eyes cry out: "We can not bear the load
> Of sighs the grievous heart sends down on us."[50]

Note the literal translation:

> You've so filled my mind with pain,
> that my soul hurries to leave,
> and the sighs my suffering heart sends
> shows my eyes it is unable to suffer.

In Pound's translation, the resulting combination of
archaic English, powerful rhythm, and precious rhyme
gives more Pound than Cavalcanti. A closer examination
will also reveal subtle changes in the original meaning.
This is not uncommon throughout Pound's Cavalcanti.
When he translates the last two lines of "Una figura della
donna mia," he is as far from Cavalcanti's literal sense as
can be. Cavalcanti writes:

> *ma dicon ch'è idolatra i Fra' Minori,*
> *per invidia che non è lor vicina.*

Pound 's version:

> 'Till brothers minor cry: "Idolatry,"
> For envy of her precious neighborhood.[51]

The literal translation:

> But the Friars Minor say it is idolatry,
> Out of Envy that she is not near them.

The difference between the two is quite clear.

Modern Analogues to Cavalcanti

Cavalcanti is undeniably universal when he suffers, but particularly modern in that he doesn't like it. We can find two interesting modern parallels to Cavalcanti in particular poems of T. S. Eliot and Tristan Tzara. For example, one of Eliot's early poems, *Portrait of a Lady*, could be seen as a twentieth-century version of the Renaissance love sonnet. One stanza reads:

Now that lilacs are in bloom
She has a bowl of lilacs in her room
And twists one in her fingers while she talks.
'Ah, my friend, you do not know, you do not know
What life is, you who hold it in your hands';
(Slowly twisting the lilac stalks)
'You let it flow from you, you let it flow,
And youth is cruel, and has no remorse
And smiles at situations which it cannot see.'[52]

Later in his maturity, in *Ash Wednesday*, Eliot amplifies similar feelings of a relationship with a lady into a much deeper sense of loss:

Lady, three white leopards sat under a juniper-tree
In the cool of the day, having fed to satiety
On my legs my heart my liver and that which had
    been contained
In the hollow round of my skull. And God said
Shall these bones live? shall these
Bones live? And that which had been contained
In the bones (which were already dry) said chirping:
Because of the goodness of this Lady
And because of her loveliness, and because
She honours the Virgin in meditation,
We shine with brightness. And I am who
    dissembled
Proffer my deeds to oblivion, and to my love

To the posterity of the desert and the fruit of the
    gourd.
It is this which recovers
My guts the strings of my eyes and the indigestible
    portions
Which leopards reject. The lady is withdrawn
In a white gown, to contemplation, in a white
gown.
Let the whiteness of bones atone to forgetfulness.
There is no life in them....[53]

Turning to the founder of the Dada movement,
Tristan Tzara, we find a poetry that is thematically simi-
lar. Tzara expresses an extreme inner dissatisfaction with
and, ultimately, a rejection of civilization and the world.
His is an expression of one gut feeling and psychological
perturbation after another. The type of self-confessed
frustration and inadequacy in *The Forbidden Fire* is com-
monplace in today's poetry, but tromped the hedges of
the well-cultivated poetic garden earlier in the century:

The night illuminated the night
the night in its wolf-traps
the waves beg from the birds
and the water fades away
since then there has been the silence
that swamps the towns apart from the dead
in silence watcher over the lamps
gnaw at the crumbs of light
without other sorrow without other silence
than the light
or a long bed of the hair of women

the eyes grow vague already the nursling's cry
neither joy nor weeping – the rocked waters
even the bears suffer from the earth
and I am always there and I have never moved
from our gamy leisures

neither hope nor lie
inventors of new magic
such magic as the world
may never more gainsay.[54]

In a stanza from Tzara's *Approximate Man,* the feeling
of self-dissolution is complete:

I speak of who speaks who is speaking I'm alone
I'm nothing but a faint noise I have several
    noises inside me
a crumpled noise frozen on the street tossed onto
the wet sidewalk
at the feet of rushing men running with their
deaths
round death stretching his arms
on the dial of the sun's only living hour.[55]

Conclusion

I hope that my translations give readers an idea of the
spontaneity and depth of Cavalcanti's poetry. He is an
essential poet for any student of poetry, history, art
history, and particularly anyone who is at all interested in
the Italian Renaissance. With powerfully frank poetic
creations revealing the stirrings of his soul, Guido
Cavalcanti is a timeless writer who has given us profound
insight into what it means to be human.

ON VERSIFICATION

Fifty-two poems have survived from Cavalcanti's oeuvre: 36 *sonetti* (sonnets), 2 *canzoni* (songs), 11 *ballate* (ballads), 1 *mottetto* (motet), and 2 *stanze isolate* (independent stanzas).

The order of the poems is that of the Ciccuto edition of Cavalcanti.[56] Cavalcanti did not intend his poems as an integral unit. They were written over the course of the maturity of his life. I have attempted to adapt my translations according to the following scheme.

Poems 1-4 mimic the Sicilian Guinisellan tradition of courtly love. I have tried to preserve some connotation of the elegant style.

Poems 5-35 are poetically innovative and thematically "pessimistic" Cavalcanti.

Poems 36-45 and 47-50 are poems of correspondence. My translations are very literal in order to preserve the historical accuracy of Cavalcanti's relationship to other poets, including Dante. Poem 46 is a *pasturella*. Sonnets 28 and 51-52 are burlesque in tone.

Before we present these poems, we will look briefly at their components: *la versa* (line or verse) and *la strofa* (the stanza).

LA VERSA

A *versa* is a determinate number of syllables in a line. In Italian, one names a verse by counting to the last accented syllable in the line and then adding one. For example, the verse:

> sull'affanoso petto

contains seven syllables and is called a *settenario*.

The verses:

> sparsa le trecce morbide

stende l'estremo vel

have respectively eight and six syllables, but they are also *settenari* because the last accented syllables are the sixth ones, to which we add one. The accented *mor-* from *morbide* is the sixth, as is the accented *vel* from the truncated *velo*.

In Italian poetry, syllables are counted in a manner different from English. Diphthongs (two vowels together in the same word) are counted as one syllable. For example, *maestro* is only two syllables even though the "ae" is two vowel sounds, or a diphthong. *Elisione, synalefe,* and *dieresi* also affect the syllable count.

Elisione (elision) is the elimination of a vowel at the end of a word for the sake of sound when the next word begins with a vowel. For example: "Chi è questa che vèn, ch'ogn'om la mira,..." The "e" of *che* and final "i" of *ogni* elide with the vowels that begin the succeeding words.

Synalefe (synalepha) is the contraction of a vowel concluding one word with the vowel beginning the next word. It is different from elision, but the result is the same: two vowels are counted as one. For example, in the verse: "e ciò che luce od è bello a vedere," the concluding vowels of *luce* and *bello* form diphthongs with the first syllable vowels of the succeeding words and are counted respectively as one syllable.

Dieresi (dieresis) is the making of two syllables from a diphthong. In the example: "fue la mia disïanza!" the "i" and "a" of *disïanza* are counted as two separate syllables, but still pronounced in the normal manner.

Italian verse types range from two to eleven syllables: *bisillabo, ternario, quaternario, quinario, senario, settenario, ottonario, novenario, decasillabo,* and *endecasillabo*.

Dante considered the *endecasillabo* the most noble, beautiful, and versatile verse of all. This eleven syllable line consists of *settenario* coupled with a *ternario, quaternario,* or a *quinario*. The choice depends on whether the coupling elides, adds, or maintains seven syllables of the *settenario*. Since each one of these three minor verses has a separate accental scheme, the *endecasillabo* has a natural rhythmical variety which lends itself to a wider array of expression than the shorter, more determinate verses.

Cavalcanti composed his *sonetti, canzoni,* and some of his *ballate* using the *endecasillabo*. As was the contemporary custom, he used the *quinario, settenario,* and *novenario* in writing his remaining *ballate* and *stanze isolate*. His *mottetto* is a scheme of irregular verses.

LA STROFA

A *strofa*, or what we call in English a stanza, consists of a certain number of verses united by a rhyming pattern. Rhyme is the matching of the vowels and consonants of two words. For example, *dolore* and *amore* rhyme, as do *maestra, finestra,* and *ginestra*.

The simplest *strofa* is the *distico,* which consists of two rhyming lines. Its rhyme pattern is AA BB CC DD. Italians refer to this as *rima baciata* (literally, kissed rhyme).

The *terzina* is a *strofa* of three verses. *Rima incatenata* has the first verse rhyme with the third, as in Dante's *Divine Comedy*. Its pattern is ABA BCB CDC DED. Cavalcanti does not use it.

The *quartina* consists of four lines rhymed ABBA *(rima incrociata)* or ABAB *(rima alternata)*. The first two *strofe* of a *sonetto* use two matching *quartine*.

A *strofa* of 5, 6, 7, 8, or 9 lines is, respectively: *quinta rima, sestina, settima rima, ottava,* or *nona rima*.

THE POETIC FORMS

When we think of older poetry today, there is a tendency to think of it as a series of rigid predetermined forms. In considering the period of early Italian poetry, nothing could be further from the truth! We should keep in mind that these poetic forms did not spring fully formed into the world of early Italian poetry. They were developed in a climate that had no hard and fast rules. For example, the Italian or Petrarchan sonnet with its classical ABBA ABBA CDE CDE form was not yet codified. Any reader who goes looking for the "proper" format of a *sonetto, ballata,* or *canzone* will be disappointed.

IL SONETTO

A sonnet is a poem of fourteen lines or verses: two *quartine* and two *terzine.* However, this format is not carved in stone. It is possible to conceptualize the *sonetto* as one *ottava* and one *sestina.* The *quartine* could be rhymed in two different patterns: ABAB ABAB or ABBA ABBA. There is even more variety in rhyming the two *terzine:* CDC CDE; CDC DCD; CDD CDD; CDE CDE; or CDE EDC *(rima invertite).* Moreover, there is a variation of the sonnet called a *sonetto caudato,* which is a regular sonnet with a *distico* added so that it totals 16 lines. There is also the *sonetto doppio* or *rinterzato,* which is used by Guido Orlandi (Poem 48B) in his response to Cavalcanti. Usually this consists of a *sestina* inserted within a regular sonnet, but Orlandi embellishes adding 8 lines instead of 6: AaBAaB AaBAaB (b)CcDdC (c)DdCcD. Cavalcanti and Orlandi wage a nasty argument in an exchange of sonnets (Poems 48A-50B). Such a poetical argument was known as *una tenzone.* Dante waged a famous *tenzone* with Forese Donati.

LA CANZONE

Dante considered the *canzone* the most noble of all poetic forms. Cavalcanti used it in his two lofty "philosophical" summations on love: "Io non pensava che lo cor giammai" (Poem 9) and "Donna me prega" (Poem 27). A *canzone* consists of a series of *strofe* called *stanze.* Some *canzoni* may conclude with a single *strofa* called a *commiato* or *congedo,* as does "Donna me prega."

The structure of a stanza varies, but it always consists of two parts: a *fronte* divided into two *piedi* and a *sirima* divided into two *volte*. The *fronte* and *sirima* may be connected with a single verse called a *chiave* or *diesis* that rhymes with the last line of the *fronte*, although Cavalcanti did not use this technique.

"Io non pensava che lo cor giammai" (Poem 9) follows the pattern: ABBC BAAC for the two *piedi* of its *fronte;* and DeD FeF for the two *volte* of the *sirima*. This poem does not conclude with a *congedo*, although "Donna me prega" does.

LA BALLATA

The *ballata* begins with a brief strofa called a *ripresa*. This is followed by two equal strofe called *mutazioni* that are followed by a *volta* or *sirima*. The last verse of the *ripresa* rhymes with the last of the *volta*. If the *ripresa* consists of only one *quinario, settenario,* or *ottonario,* it is a *ballata minima;* if one *endecasillabo,* a *ballata piccola;* if two verses, a *ballata minore;* if three verses, a *ballata mezzana* or *media;* and if four or more verses, a *ballata stravagante.*

Although medieval poetry is closely connected to music, the *ballata* is the only one of the literary Italian forms that might be performed musically. While a soloist sang the *stanze,* the chorus would dance around him in a circle and sing the *ripresa* at the end of each *stanza*. The *ballata stravagante* "Vedete ch'i son un che vo piangendo" (Poem 10) contains a *ripresa* with internal rhymes in the pattern Z(W)XX(W)Y, two *strofe* or *mutazioni* of AB AB and a *volta* or *sirima* of BXXY.

There is an excellent explanation of *stilnovisti* versification in volume 1 of Foster and Boyd's *Dante's Lyric Poetry,* 2 vols. (London: Oxford University Press, 1967). For those who read Italian, the following are very illuminating: Mario Fubini, *Metrica e poesia Lezioni sulle forme metriche italiane* I. *Dal Duecento al Petrarca* (Milan:

Feltrinelli, 1962); Silvana Ghiazza, *Elementi di metrica italiana e cenni di retorica* (Bari: Levante, 1985); and Enrico Bianchi, *Retorica e metrica italiana* (Florence: Le Monnier, 1962).

NOTES

1. For complete editions of Cavalcanti's poetry, see Guido Cavalcanti, *Rime*, edited by Marcello Ciccuto with an introduction by Maria Corti (Milan: Rizzoli Editore, 1978). This particular edition is based on Gianfranco Contini, *Poeti del duecento* (Milan-Naples: Riccardo Riccardi, 1960), 2:487-567. Contini's Cavalcanti is an update of the standard critical edition by G. Favati, *Le rime* (Milan-Naples: Riccardo Riccardi, 1957). Favati provides copious philological notes on manuscript sources for the poems. There is a recent literal translation of Cavalcanti's poetry by Lowry Nelson, Jr., *The Poetry of Guido Cavalcanti* (New York: Garland Publishing, 1986). Ciccuto and Nelson each provide comprehensive bibliographies on Cavalcanti.
2. Robert Haas, *Twentieth Century Pleasures* (New York: Ecco Press, 1984), p. 109.
3. Benedetto Croce, *Aesthetica in nuce* (Bari: Laterza, 1979), p. 9. This is the Italian version of the article that Croce wrote on "Aesthetics" for the fourteenth edition of the *Encyclopedia Britannica.*
4. The following historical section is based on two excellent modern studies: William Anderson, *Dante the Maker* (New York: Crossroad, 1982), ch. 10; and Giorgio Petrocchi, *La Vita di Dante,* (Bari: Laterza, 1986), ch. 9; as well as two primary sources: Dino Compagni, *Cronica,* (Milan: Rizzoli, 1965); and Filippo Villani, *Le vite d'uomini illustri fiorentini,* ed. G. M. Mazzuchelli (Florence: Sansone Coen, 1847).
5. For Dante's early education, see Anderson, *Dante the Maker,* pp. 70-75; Francesco Maggini, *Introduzione allo studio di Dante* (Pisa: Nistri-Lischi, 1965), pp. 19-21; and Petrocchi, *Vita di Dante,* chs. 2 and 3. For the poets mentioned in Dante's writing, see Teolinda Barolini, *Dante's Poets: Textuality and Truth in the Comedy* (Princeton: Princeton University Press, 1984), esp. the appendix, pp. 287-97; and p. 92 n. 9. For more precise information on late medieval and Renaissance educational practices and curricula in Italy and Europe, and the influence of spirituial trends, see

Charles T. Davis, "Education in Dante's Florence," *Speculum* 40, 3 (1965): 415-35; and the articles and bibliography in Paul F. Grendler, ed., "Education in the Renaissance and Reformation," *Renaissance Quarterly* 43, 4 (1990): 774-824.

6. Giorgio Petrocchi, "Il Dolce stil nuovo," *Storia della letteratura italiana: Le origini e il Duecento* (Milan: Garzanti, 1965), 1:750.

7. Alfredo Schiaffini provides a clear, scholarly discussion of the Provençal, Sicilian, Tuscan connection in the development of the love lyric and the poetic language of Italy during this period in his "La prima elaborazione della forma poetica italiana," *Momenti di storia della lingua italiana* (Rome: Editrice Studium, 1965), pp. 7-42.

8. There is a very sound treatment of the influence of Guinizelli's canzone in Frederick Goldin, *German and Italian Lyrics of the Middle Ages* (New York: Anchor Books, 1973), pp. 280-85.

9. The poetry of the troubadours is covered completely in Maurice Valency, *In Praise of Love* (New York: Octagon Books, 1975); L. T. Topsfield, *The Troubadours and Love* (Cambridge: Cambridge University Press, 1975); and Peter Dronke, *The Medieval Lyric* (New York: Cambridge University Press, 1977). For a further examination of the Provençal lyricists as well as fine translations of their poems, the reader should consult Meg Bogin, *The Women Troubadours* (New York: Paddington Press, 1976); and Frederick Goldin, *Lyrics of the Troubadours and Trouveres* (New York: Anchor Books, 1973). Flavio Catenazzi provides a very detailed examination of thematic sources of the Provençal troubadours used by their Sicilian and Tuscan counterparts in his *L'influsso dei provenzali sui temi e immagini della poesia siculo-toscana* (Brescia: Morcelliana, 1977).

10. There is extensive literature on the art of courtly love and chivalry. For some traditional as well as more current views, see Sidney Painter, *French Chivalry* (Ithaca, NY: Cornell University Press, 1974, reprint of 1940 edition); Carl Stephenson, *Feudalism* (Ithaca, NY: Cornell University Press, 1979, reprint of 1942 edition); C. Stephen Jaeger, *The Origins of Courtliness* (Philadelphia: University of Pennsylvania Press, 1985); and *In Pursuit of Perfection,* an anthology edited by Joan M. Ferrante and George D. Economou (Port Washington, NY: Kennikat Press, 1975); William D. Paden, ed., *The Voice of the Trobairitz* (Philadelphia: University of Pennsylvania Press, 1989); and Roger Boase, *The Origin and Meaning of Courtly Love* (Manchester: The University Press, 1977).

11.   Valency, *In Praise,* p. 195, explains: "The Italians did more than extend a welcome to the jongleurs from France. With typical enthusiasm, they seized upon the literary baggage of these visitors, and made it their own. In an incredibly short time the paladins of Charlemagne were naturalized in Italy, and their doings, endlessly supplemented and embroidered, remained a matter of concern to the Italians long after the taste for these stories had spent itself in France. The Provençal love-poetry, similarly, took root firmly in the Italian cities, and, shedding its original language little by little, it became Italian."

12.   Paul Oskar Kristeller makes the observation that the *stilnovisti* were more philosophical than their French predecessors in his "Humanism and Moral Philosophy," *Renaissance Humanism: Foundations, Forms and Legacy,* ed. by Albert Rabil, Jr. (Philadelphia: University of Pennsylvania Press, 1988), 3:294. For further discussion, see note 21.

13.   On the point of numbers in commerce and art, see Michael Baxandall, *Painting and Experience in Fifteenth Century Italy* (New York: Oxford University Press, 1974). For a discussion of the significance of numerical proportion in Renaissance philosophy and architecture, see Rudolph Wittkower, *Renaissance Architectural Principles in the Age of Humanism* (New York: W.W. Norton, 1971).

14.   *Convivio,* 2.12-13, taken from the anthology translated and edited by Robert S. Haller, *Literary Criticism of Dante Alighieri* (Lincoln, NE: University of Nebraska Press, 1973), p. 114.

15.   A classic study on the development of medieval allegorical reading is Beryl Smalley, *The Study of the Bible in the Middle Ages,* (Oxford: Basil Blackwell, 1984 [1952]).

16.   Haller, *Literary Criticism of Dante,* p. xl.

17.   C. S. Lewis, *The Allegory of Love* (Oxford: Oxford University Press, 1936), pp. 60-61.

18.   "In the literature of the fourteenth century, the warrior plays a smaller role....The fighting champion of the Heroic Age has become the 'officer and gentleman' of the modern world." *The Norton Anthology of World Masterpieces,* ed. Maynard Mack (New York: W.W. Norton, 1985), 1:1025-26.

19.   José Ortega y Gasset, *The Revolt of the Masses* (New York: W.W. Norton, 1932), pp. 75-76.

20.   Ortega, *Revolt,* p. 63.

21.   The link between poeticizing about love and philosophically investigating its nature is certain. Dante, Cavalcanti, and other

stilnovisti had a direct intellectual link with a philosopher on the arts faculty at the University of Bologna, Giacomo da Pistoia. Pistoia dedicates his treatise on love, *Questio de felicitate,* to Cavalcanti. This intellectual inquiry regarding the nature, scope, and origin of happiness ultimately dealt with the science of the human soul, or what we today call psychology. See Maria Corti, *La felicità mentale. Nuove prospettive per Cavalcanti e Dante* (Turin: Einaudi, 1983), pp. 5-8. The origin of Corti's conclusions come from Paul Oskar Kristeller's essay on, and publication of, Pistoia's essay in "A Philosophical Treatise from Bologna Dedicated to Guido Cavalcanti: Magister Jacobus de Pistorio and His 'Questio de felicitate'," in *Medioevo e Rinascimento. Studi in onore di Bruno Nardi* (Florence: Sansoni, 1955), pp. 425-63.

22. Dante, *De Vulgari Eloquentia* (I, 16), trans. Sally Purcell (Manchester: Carcant New Press, 1981), p. 35.

23. *De Monarchia,* from *A Translation of the Latin Works of Dante Alighieri,* A. G. Ferrers Howell and Phillip H. Wicksteed, trans. (London: J.M. Dent, 1904; reprint, Ann Arbor, MI: University Microfilms, 1975), p. 133.

24. Carlo Salinari makes the perceptive observation that the poets of the court of Frederick II "...transferred all the problems that daily life posed to a spiritual and universal code....And love, a universal sentiment, became the junction in which experiences of life, cultural needs, ideological proposals, and attitudes of taste intertwined – all which represented the labors of an entire civilization and the human condition of an epoch...." See his prefatory essay to the anthology *La poesia lirica del Duecento* (Turin: UTET, 1968), p. 14.

25. Guido Cavalcanti, "Una giovane donna di Tolosa," *Rime,* ed. Ciccuto, p. 127. The poetic translation is mine. See below, pp. 73-75.

26. Mario Marti, *Con Dante fra i poeti del suo tempo* (Lecce: Milella, 1971), pp. 161-62.

27. My subsequent discussion of Cavalcanti's Averroism is based on Bruno Nardi, *Dante e la cultura medievale* (Rome: Editori Laterza, 1983).

28. Irwin Panofsky, "Blind Cupid," in *Studies in Iconology,* (New York: Harper & Row, 1967), pp. 101-2. Panofsky emphasizes that some medieval portraits of Love do not depict the little pagan Cupid but build visionary allegories of exalted, metaphysical love constructed from sources in classical literature and medieval scholarship (pp. 97-99).

29. Nardi, *Dante e la cultura medievale,* pp. 30-32. With another point of view, Thomas Hyde, *The Poetic Theology of Love,* (Newark, DE: University of Delaware Press, 1986), pp. 29-30, stresses that although Cavalcanti's *Amore* might seem to possess supernatural powers, there is a medieval ambiguity concerning Love (or Cupid) that keeps him in "a limbo between true divinity and personification." For the poetic inception of Guido's personifications, see the notes to Poems 5, 6, and 9.

30. Francesco De Sanctis, that wonderful nineteenth-century critic, praised Cavalcanti as "the first Italian poet worthy of this title, because he is the first who had the sense and sensibility of the real." In other words, Cavalcanti discarded the formulaic conventions of earlier love poetry in favor of lyricizing the reality he observed. See his *Storia della letteratura italiana* (Milan: Rizzoli, 1983), 1:110.

31. *De Vulgari Eloquentia,* (I, 1), trans. Purcell, p. 15.

32. For all the talk among critics of the "aristocratic" nature of the *dolce stil nuovo,* there were never more simple and common words written in poetry than the lines beginning the poem that culminates this entire sphere of poetry:

> *Nel mezzo del cammin di nostra vita*
> *mi ritrovai per una selva oscura,*
> *chè la diritta via era smarita. (Inferno,* I, 1-3)

> In the middle of the walk of our life
> I found myself in a dark wood,
> because the correct path was lost.

33. *De Vulgari Eloquentia,* (I, 17), trans. Purcell, pp. 34-35.

34. Erich Auerbach, *Literary Language and Its Public in Late Latin Antiquity and in the Middle Ages,* trans. Ralph Manheim (New York: Pantheon Books, 1965), p. 220.

35. Auerbach, *Literary Language,* esp. pp. 47-66.

36. Schiaffini, "A proposito dello stile comico di Dante," *Momenti di Storia,* pp. 43-56, quotes from pp. 49-50.

37. Petrocchi, *Vita di Dante,* p. 72.

38. Auerbach, *Literary Language,* pp. 223-23; and Gianfranco Contini, *Rime di Dante* (Turin: Einaudi, 1965), pp. 165-66. Contini points out that as he develops as a poet, Dante contrasts *asprezza* (harshness) with the *lenitas* (smoothness) of his earlier work, thereby giving his work a wider range of expression.

39. Alfredo Schiaffini, "La prima elaborazione," *Momenti di storia,* pp. 7-42.

40. Bruno Migliorini, *Storia della lingua italiana* (Florence: Sansoni, 1983), p. 137. See also the English translation, *The Italian Language,* ed. T. Gwynfor Griffith (London: Faber & Faber, 1984), ch. 4.

41. Schiaffini, "La prima elaborazione," pp. 20-22.

42. Migliorini, *Storia della lingua,* pp. 129-30. Although there was a common poetic vocabulary developing at this time, Dante erroneously concluded that there was an Italian language common to much of Italy regardless of the extreme dialectical differences. He arrived at this opinion by studying the poetry of Sicily as copied by Tuscan amanuenses, not realizing that they had changed many of the words into Tuscan or, at least, Tuscanized them. On this point, see Francesco D'Ovidio, *Versificazione italiana e arte poetica medioevale* (Milan: Hoepli, 1910), pp. 521-25.

43. Petrocchi, "Il Dolce stil nuovo," 1:756-57, observes that Cavalcanti's poetic gift manifests itself in a "refined language, rich in verbal music and expressive perfection, capable, at times, of effective realistic images, of a raw power that we will find only in Dante." He considers Poems 20, 22, 32, 33, and 34 among his best, with Poem 35 at the summit with its "delicate grief...where suffering is ever more purified in poetry...."

44. Italian text of Lapo Gianni, "Dolc'è 'l pensier," lines 21-24, from *German and Italian Lyrics,* ed. Goldin, p. 340. My own translation.

45. Italo Calvino refers to Cavalcanti's poetry as "lightness" in comparison to Dante's, which he considers to possess "weight." See his *Six Memos for the Next Millennium* (Cambridge: Harvard University Press, 1988), ch. 1. He seems to miss the dramatic quality of Guido's verse. Calvino admires the determination and precision of Cavalcanti's poetry. For a discussion of Cavalcanti's dramatic quality, see Maria Corti's introduction to Guido Cavalcanti, *Rime,* pp. 5-27.

46. Dante Gabriel Rossetti, *The Early Italian Poets,* ed. Sally Purcell (Berkeley, CA: University of California Press, 1982), p. 222.

47. Schiaffini, "A proposito di Dante," pp. 48-50. E. G. Parodi explains that Dante was not a forced or unscrupulous poet when he "borrowed" so creatively. Many poets did, but not with Dante's attempt to systematize this hybridism. On the one hand, Latin grammar provided the system, while on the other, the vernaculars provided the great variety and free movements. See "La rima e i

vocaboli nella *Divina Commedia,*" *Lingua e letteratura* (Venice: Neri Pozza, 1957), pp. 204-21.

48. In copying manuscripts of Sicilian poetry, Tuscan amanuenses transform their native *io* and the Sicilian *eu* into an *eo*, a sort of intermediary between the two dialects. See Ireneo Sanesi, "Il toscaneggiamento della poesia siciliana," *Giornale storico della letteratura Italiana* 34 (1899): 359.

49. Ezra Pound, "The 'Introduction' to Sonnets and Ballate," from *Pound's Cavalcanti,* ed. David Anderson (Princeton: Princeton University Press, 1983), p. 19.

50. Ibid., p. 39.

51. Ibid., p. 123.

52. T. S. Eliot, "Portrait of a Lady," *Selected Poems* (New York: Harcourt Brace, 1964), p. 18.

53. Eliot, "Ash Wednesday," *Selected Poems,* p. 85.

54. Translation of "Le feu defendu" by Cecily Mackworth from her *A Mirror for French Poetry 1840-1940* (London: George Routledge and Sons, 1947), p. 191.

55. Translation of Tzara's "L'homme approximatif" by Paul Auster is found in *The Random House Book of Twentieth-Century French Poetry,* ed. Paul Auster (New York: Random House, 1982), p. 175.

56. See n. 1 above.

GUIDO CAVALCANTI
THE COMPLETE POEMS

I

Fresca rosa novella,
piacente primavera,
per prata e per rivera
gaiamente cantando,
vostro fin presio mando – a la verdura.   5

    Lo vostro presio fino
in gio' si rinovelli
da grandi e da zitelli
per ciascuno camino;
    e cantin[n]e gli auselli   10
ciascuno in suo latino
da sera e da matino
su li verdi arbuscelli.
    Tutto lo mondo canti,
po' che lo tempo vène,   15
sì come si convene,
vostr'altezza presiata:
ché siete angelicata – crïatura.

    Angelica sembranza
in voi, donna, riposa: 20
Dio, quanto aventurosa
fue la mia disïanza!
    Vostra cera gioiosa,
poi che passa e avanza
natura e costumanza,   25
ben è mirabil cosa.

I

my young blossom
renascent beauty
among the country meadows
singing joyfully
i commend your worth – to the greenery

    let men and boys
joyously repeat
your value
on every walkway
    let the birds sing
each in his clarity
from dawn to dusk
from the verdant trees
    let the world sing
at the turn of spring
as it must be
your spiritual value
for you've become an angel – sweet creature

    angelic semblance
rests in you, Lady:
God, how lucky
was my desire!
    your joyous countenance
surpassing and transcending
nature and birthright
ah, so admirable

Fra lor le donne dea
vi chiaman, come sète;
tanto adorna parete,
ch'eo non saccio contare;   30
e chi poria pensare – oltra natura?

Oltra natura umana
vostra fina piasenza
fece Dio, per essenza
che voi foste sovrana: 35
   per che vostra parvenza
ver' me non sia luntana;
or non mi sia villana
la dolce provedenza!
   E se vi pare oltraggio   40
ch' ad amarvi sia dato,
non sia da voi blasmato:
ché solo Amor mi sforza,
contra cui non val forza – né misura.

among themselves women call you
goddess, for you are
so complete, you
i don't know how to explain
and who could think – beyond nature?

beyond human nature
God made your
fine grace, in essence
that you would be sovereign:
so you in truth
won't be far from me –
don't be rude to me
sweet providence
and if it appears offensive
that i'm devoted to loving you
don't blame me
as only love moves me
against whom succeeds neither force nor limits.

2

Avete 'n vo' li fior' e la verdura
e ciò che luce od è bello a vedere;
risplende più che sol vostra figura:
chi vo' non vede, ma' non pò valere.

In questo mondo non ha creatura   5
sì piena di bieltà né di piacere;
e chi d'amor si teme, lu' assicura
vostro bel vis' a tanto 'n sé volere.

Le donne che vi fanno compagnia
assa' mi piaccion per lo vostro amore;   10
ed i' le prego per lor cortesia

che qual più può più vi faccia onore
ed aggia cara vostra segnoria,
perché di tutte siete la migliore.

2

in you flowers and greenery
and beautiful light
shine more than the sun
who doesn't want to see you, can't appreciate

in this world no creature
is filled with your beauty and charm
and who fears love is reassured
in his desire by your beautiful face

the ladies in your company
delight me because of your love
so i ask their courtesy

so whoever can honor you more, do so
and have your noble attention
because you are the best of all

3

Biltà di donna e di saccente core
e cavalieri armati che sien genti;
cantar d'augelli e ragionar d'amore;
adorni legni 'n mar forte correnti;

aria serena quand' apar l'albore   5
e bianca neve scender senza venti;
rivera d'acqua e prato d'ogni fiore;
oro, argento, azzuro 'n ornamenti:

ciò passa la beltate e la valenza
de la mia donna e 'l su' gentil coraggio,   ·   10
sì che rasembra vile a chi ciò guarda;

e tanto più d'ogn' altr' ha canoscenza,
quanto lo ciel de la terra è maggio.
A simil di natura ben non tarda.

3

beauty of women and wise hearts
and noble armed cavaliers
birds' song and love's reason
bedecked ships in strong seas

serene air at dawn
and white snow falling windlessly
watery brooks and fields of all flowers
gold, silver, lapis lazuli in adornment:

these are transcended by the beauty and grace
of my Lady and her gentle heart
which renders unworthy he who looks at her

and she is wiser than anyone
as the heavens are greater than the earth
to such a similar nature, goodness delays not

4

Chi è questa che vèn, ch'ogn'om la mira,
che fa tremar di chiaritate l'àre
e mena seco Amor, sì che parlare
null'omo pote, ma ciascun sospira?

O Deo, che sembra quando li occhi gira,   5
dical' Amor, ch'i' nol savria contare:
cotanto d'umiltà donna mi pare,
ch'ogn'altra ver' di lei i' la chiam' ira.

Non si poria contar la sua piagenza,
ch'a le' s'inchin' ogni gentil vertute,   10
e la beltate per sua dea la mostra.

Non fu sì alta già la mente nostra
e non si pose 'n noi tanta salute,
che propiamente n'aviàn conoscenza.

4

who is this who came
who makes the air tremble with purity
and leads love, so no man
may speak, but only sigh

Oh God, who appears when eyes turn
speak of her, Love, as i can't:
she seems of such humility
that others compared to her seem Furies

one can't sing of her beauty
to which other noble virtues kneel
and beauty shows her as its goddess

our minds were never so heightened
and we never had such salvation
that we could really know her

5

Li mie' foll' occhi, che prima guardaro
vostra figura piena di valore,
fuor quei che di voi, donna, m'acusaro
nel fero loco ove ten corte Amore,

e mantinente avanti lui mostraro   5
ch' io era fatto vostro servidore:
per che sospiri e dolor mi pigliaro,
vedendo che temenza avea lo core.

Menârmi tosto, sanza riposanza,
in una parte là 'v' i' trovai gente   10
che ciascun si doleva d'Amor forte.

Quando mi vider, tutti con pietanza
dissermi: "Fatto se', di tal, servente,
che mai non déi sperare altro che morte."

5

my foolish eyes, that first looked
at your worth
without yours knowing, Lady, condemned me
in that fierce place where Love holds court

and suddenly before him they showed
i was your servant:
thus sighs and pain took me
seeing the fear in my heart

leading me quickly without pause
to a place where i found nobles
who suffered strongly from love

when they saw me, all with pity
said to me – you've been made a servant –
you must never hope for anything but death

6

Deh, spiriti miei, quando mi vedete
con tanta pena, come non mandate
fuor della mente parole adornate
di pianto, dolorose e sbigottite?

Deh, voi vedete che 'l core ha ferite   5
di sguardo e di piacer e d'umiltate:
deh, i' vi priego che voi 'l consoliate
che son da lui le sue vertù partite.

I' veggo a luï spirito apparire
alto e gentile e di tanto valore,   10
che fa le sue vertù tutte fuggire.

Deh, i' vi priego che deggiate dire
a l'alma trista, che parl' in dolore,
com' ella fu e fie sempre d'Amore.

6

alas, my spirits, when you see me
in such pain, why doesn't your intellect
send words adorned
in tears, painful and despondent

alas, you see my heart is wounded
from glances and pleasure and submission:
alas, i beg you console him
for his virtues have left

i see a spirit appear to him
lofty and gentle and so worthy
that makes his virtues flee

alas, i pray that you must sing
to a sad soul, who painfully speaks –
as he was and will be – of Love

7

L'anima mia vilment' è sbigotita
de la battaglia ch'e[l]l'ave dal core:
che s'ella sente pur un poco Amore
più presso a lui che non sòle, ella more.

Sta come quella che non ha valore,   5
ch'è per temenza da lo cor partita;
e chi vedesse com' ell' è fuggita
diria per certo: "Questi non ha vita."

Per li occhi venne la battaglia in pria,
che ruppe ogni valore immantenente,   10
sì che del colpo fu strutta la mente.

Qualunqu' è quei che più allegrezza sente,
se vedesse li spirti fuggir via,
di grande sua pietate piangeria.

7

my soul is wildly terrified
of the battle within my heart:
because if it feels even a little Love
within one not used to it, it dies

remaining as one with no value
that has – for fear – left my heart
and whoever would see this exodus
would certainly say – no life here –

first into the eyes came the battle
that immediately broke every virtue
so that my mind was destroyed

whoever has rapture the more
sees his spirits run away
loudly crying out his grief

8

Tu m'hai sì piena di dolor la mente,
che l'anima si briga di partire,
e li sospir' che manda 'l cor dolente
mostrano agli occhi che non può soffrire.

Amor, che lo tuo grande valor sente,   5
dice: "E' mi duol che ti convien morire
per questa fiera donna, che nïente
par che piatate di te voglia udire."

I' vo come colui ch'è fuor di vita,
che pare, a chi lo sguarda, ch'omo sia   10
fatto di rame o di pietra o di legno,

che si conduca sol per maestria
e porti ne lo core una ferita
che sia, com'egli è morto, aperto segno.

8

you've so filled my mind with pain
my soul hurries to leave
my heart moans to my eyes
it can suffer no more

Love, feeling your worth,
says – I'm sad you must die
by this fiery woman, who flat
refuses to hear of your mercy –

i walk as dead
appearing – to who will look – a man
made of bronze or stone or wood

crafted by her mastery
with a wounded heart
active mortality, an open sign

9

Io non pensava che lo cor giammai
avesse di sospir' tormento tanto,
che dell'anima mia nascesse pianto
mostrando per lo viso agli occhi morte.
    Non sentìo pace né riposo alquanto   5
poscia ch'Amore e madonna trovai,
lo qual mi disse: "Tu non camperai,
ché troppo è lo valor di costei forte."
    La mia virtù si partìo sconsolata
poi che lassò lo core   10
a la battaglia ove madonna è stata:
    la qual degli occhi suoi venne a ferire
in tal guisa, ch'Amore
ruppe tutti miei spiriti a fuggire.

    Di questa donna non si può contare: 15
ché di tante bellezze adorna vène,
che mente di qua giù no la sostene
sì che la veggia lo 'ntelletto nostro.
    Tant' è gentil che, quand' eo penso bene,
l'anima sento per lo cor tremare,   20
sì come quella che non pò durare
davanti al gran valor ch'è i·llei dimostro.
    Per gli occhi fere la sua claritate,
sì che quale mi vede
dice: "Non guardi tu questa pietate   25
    ch'è posta invece di persona morta
per dimandar merzede?"
E non si n'è madonna ancor accorta!

9

i never used to think that my heart
could have such tormented laments
that my soul would be born crying
revealing a face with dead eyes
i felt neither peace nor even rest
in the place where i found love and my Lady –
who said to me – you won't escape
because my strength is too great –
my ability left disconsolate
since my heart abandoned
the battle over my Lady
whose eyes came to wound
in such a guise that Love
broke my spirits into fleeing

of her one couldn't sing
other than her coming in a beauty
that our lowly minds couldn't sustain
what our intellects saw
so gentle is she that when she fills my mind
my soul feels my heart shiver
so it can't continue
before her worthiness
her purity blinds my eyes
so that those seeing me
say – isn't your looking at this grace
like the task of those dead
seeking forgiveness? –
and one is no longer aware of my Lady!

Quando 'l pensier mi vèn ch'i' voglia dire
a gentil core de la sua vertute, 30
i' trovo me di sì poca salute,
ch'i' non ardisco di star nel pensero.
  Amor, c'ha le bellezze sue vedute,
mi sbigottisce sì, che sofferire
non può lo cor sentendola venire, 35
ché sospirando dice: "Io ti dispero,
    però che trasse del su' dolce riso
una saetta aguta,
c'ha passato 'l tuo core e 'l mio diviso.
  Tu sai, quando venisti, ch'io ti dissi, 40
poi che l'avéi veduta,
per forza convenia che tu morissi."

  Canzon, tu sai che de' libri d'Amore
io t'asemplai quando madonna vidi:
ora ti piaccia ch'io di te mi fidi 45
e vadi 'n guis' a lei, ch'ella t'ascolti;
    e prego umilemente a lei tu guidi
li spiriti fuggiti del mio core,
che per soverchio de lo su' valore
eran distrutti, se non fosser vòlti, 50
    e vanno soli, senza compagnia,
e son pien' di paura.
Però li mena per fidata via
    e poi le di', quando le se' presente:
"Questi sono in figura 55
d'un che si more sbigottitamente."

when a thought comes to me i want to tell
a gentle heart of her virtue
i find myself with little strength
that i dare not remain in such mind
Love, she is a vision of beauty
that terrifies me, my heart
suffers her approach
as he sighs – i deprive you of hope
drawing from her sweet smile
a sharp arrow
piercing your heart and dividing mine
you know when you approached i said
since you have seen her
you are forced to die –

    Canzon, you know the books of Love
i copied when i saw my Lady:
now you want me to trust you
and go to her in a way that she'll listen
then i humbly ask you to guide
the return of the spirits that fled
my heart because they were destroyed by
the crush of her power as if they had no courage
wandering alone without companionship
afraid
so lead them to salvation
and tell her, when she is present –
these belonged to one
who died wretchedly –

IO

Vedete ch'i' son un che vo piangendo
e dimostrando – il giudicio d'Amore,
e già non trovo sì pietoso core
che, me guardando, – una volta sospiri.

    Novella doglia m'è nel cor venuta,   5
la qual mi fa doler e pianger forte;
    e spesse volte avèn che mi saluta
tanto di presso l'angosciosa Morte,
    che fa 'n quel punto le persone accorte,
che dicono infra lor: "Quest' ha dolore,   10
e già, secondo che ne par de fòre,
dovrebbe dentro aver novi martiri."

    Questa pesanza ch'è nel cor discesa
ha certi spirite' già consumati,
    i quali eran venuti per difesa   15
del cor dolente che gli avea chiamati.
    Questi lasciaro gli occhi abbandonati
quando passò nella mente un romore
il qual dicea: "Dentro, Biltà, ch'e' more;
ma guarda che Pietà non vi si miri!"   20

10

you see me – one who goes crying
an example to all of Love's judgment
and i don't find a pitying heart
sigh even once looking at me

    fresh sorrow came in my heart
so making me ache and cry
    often and nearby
tormenting Death greeted me
    just then telling others
who say to each other – this one suffers
and already beside himself
inside he should be martyred –

    this sorrow descended in my heart
already consuming certain spirits
    which came to defend
my sorrowing heart's plea
    they abandoned my eyes
when a noise passed through my mind
saying – inside, Beauty, he dies
so beware Pity doesn't see you

II

Poi che di doglia cor conven ch'i' porti
e senta di piacere ardente foco
e di virtù mi traggi' a sì vil loco,
dirò com'ho perduto ogni valore.
    E dico che' miei spiriti son morti,   *5*
e 'l cor che tanto ha guerra e vita poco;
e se non fosse che 'l morir m'è gioco,
fare'ne di pietà pianger Amore.

    Ma, per lo folle tempo che m'ha giunto,
mi cangio di mia ferma oppinïone   *10*
in altrui condizione,
sì ch'io non mostro quant'io sento affanno:
là 'nd'eo ricevo inganno,
ché dentro da lo cor mi pass' Amanza,
che se ne porta tutta mia possanza.   *15*

11

since i must bear a sorrowing heart
and feel pleasure's burning fire
and virtue drag me down
i'll tell of losing all virtue
    and i'll tell of my spirits dying
and a heart with little life but much strife
and if death weren't a game to me
i'd make Love cry with mercy

    but in this foolish moment
i change from decisiveness
to another state
so i won't show my grief:
there where i find deceit
since Love pierced my heart
carrying away all my power

12

Perché non fuoro a me gli occhi dispenti
o tolti, sì che de la lor veduta
non fosse nella mente mia venuta
a dir: "Ascolta se nel cor mi senti?"

Ch'una paura di novi tormenti   5
m'aparve allor, sì crudel e aguta,
che l'anima chiamò: "Donna, or ci aiuta,
che gli occhi ed i' non rimagnàn dolenti!

Tu gli ha' lasciati sì, che venne Amore
a pianger sovra lor pietosamente,   10
tanto che s'ode una profonda voce

la quale dice: – Chi gran pena sente
guardi costui, e vedrà 'l su' core
che Morte 'l porta 'n man tagliato in croce –."

12

why weren't my eyes blinded
or taken so that their visions
weren't in my mind
to say – listen if you feel me in your heart –

that a shudder of new torments
appear to me – so cruel and sharp –
that my soul calls out – Woman help
my eyes not to suffer

so left bereft that Love came
to weep over them
that a deep voice was heard

to say – whoever suffers such
look at him and see his heart
carried by Death's hand– carved into a cross

13

Voi che per li occhi mi passaste 'l core
e destaste la mente che dormia,
guardate a l'angosciosa vita mia,
che sospirando la distrugge Amore.

E' vèn tagliando di sì gran valore,   5
che' deboletti spiriti van via:
riman figura sol en segnoria
e voce alquanta, che parla dolore.

Questa vertù d'amor che m'ha disfatto
da' vostr' occhi gentil' presta si mosse: 10
un dardo mi gittò dentro dal fianco.

Sì giunse ritto 'l colpo al primo tratto,
che l'anima tremando si riscosse
veggendo morto 'l cor nel lato manco.

13

you who've pierced my eyes to my heart
awakening my sleeping mind
look at my anguished life
sighing, destroyed by Love

cut with such force
weakened spirits flee:
one remains in dominion
a weak voice in pain

Love's virtue undid me
quickly from your noble eyes:
an arrow pierced my side

bull's eye direct on the first try
shaking my trembling soul
seeing my dead heart in my left side's hole

14

Se m'ha del tutto oblïato Merzede,
già però Fede – il cor non abandona,
anzi ragiona – di servire a grato
al dispietato – core.
    E, qual sì sente simil me, ciò crede;   5
ma chi tal vede – (certo non persona),
ch'Amor mi dona – un spirito 'n su' stato
che figurato, – more?
    Ché, quando lo piacer mi stringe tanto
che lo sospir si mova,   10
par che nel cor mi piova
un dolce amor sì bono
ch'eo dico: "Donna, tutto vostro sono."

14

if you've forgotten me forever, Mercy
at least my heart doesn't abandon Faith
but thinks of freely serving
a pitiless heart
    and he who feels as i believes such
but who sees – certainly no one else –
that Love gives me a spirit in a state
that, as such, dies
    so when pleasure grips me so tight
agitating sighs
it seems my heart cries
a sweet love so good
i say – Lady, i'm all yours

15

Se Mercé fosse amica a' miei disiri,
e 'l movimento suo fosse dal core
di questa bella donna, [e] 'l su' valore
mostrasse la vertute a' mie' martiri,

d'angosciosi dilett' i miei sospiri,   5
che nascon della mente ov'è Amore
e vanno sol ragionando dolore
e non trovan persona che li miri,

giriano agli occhi con tanta vertute,
che 'l forte e 'l duro lagrimar che fanno   10
ritornerebbe in allegrezza e 'n gioia.

Ma sì è al cor dolente tanta noia
e all'anima trista è tanto danno,
che per disdegno uom non dà lor salute.

15

if only Mercy befriended my desires
and moved from the heart
of this beautiful woman, and her worth
would show virtue to my torments and

my sighs of anguishing pleasure
born in my mind where Love resides
alone reasoning pain
unseen by others

would enter my eyes virtuously
so their strong and sturdy tears
would change to happiness and joy –

but such irks my grieving heart
and harms my sad soul
that out of disdain no one greets them

16

A me stesso di me pietate vène
per la dolente angoscia ch'i' mi veggio:
di molta debolezza quand'io seggio,
l'anima sento ricoprir di pene.

Tutto mi struggo, perch'io sento bene   *5*
che d'ogni angoscia la mia vita è peggio;
la nova donna cu' merzede cheggio
questa battaglia di dolor' mantene:

però che, quand' i' guardo verso lei,
rizzami gli occhi dello su' disdegno   *10*
sì feramente, che distrugge 'l core.

Allor si parte ogni vertù da' miei
e 'l cor si ferma per veduto segno
dove si lancia crudeltà d'amore.

16

pity came to lonely me
in my self-anguish:
sitting in my weakness
i feel my soul blanketed in pain

everything destroys me – as i feel
each anguish my life is worse
the young woman whose mercy i ask
keeps up the battle:

when i look towards her
her eyes laugh with a disdain
so fierce it destroys my heart

then all my virtues leave
and my heart stops – becoming a target
for Love's cruel lance

17

S'io prego questa donna che Pietate
non sia nemica del su' cor gentile,
tu di' ch'i' sono sconoscente e vile
e disperato e pien di vanitate.

Onde ti vien sì nova crudeltate?   5
Già risomigli, a chi ti vede, umìle,
saggia e adorna e accorta e sottile
e fatta a modo di soavitate!

L'anima mia dolente e paurosa
piange ne li sospir' che nel cor trova,   10
sì che bagnati di pianti escon fòre.

Allora par che ne la mente piova
una figura di donna pensosa
che vegna per veder morir lo core.

17

if i ask Pity not to be
an enemy of this Lady's gentle heart
you call me ungrateful and vile
and desperate and vain

where do you get such cruelty?
you seem – to those seeing you – humble
wise, complete, prudent, subtle
and with manner sweet!

my sorrowing and fearful soul
wails in my sighing heart
until tears extinguish it

then crying in my mind
a melancholy Lady
comes to see my heart die

18

Noi siàn le triste pene isbigotite,
le cesoiuzze e 'l coltellin dolente,
ch'avemo scritte dolorosamente
quelle parole che vo' avete udite.

Or vi diciàn perché noi siàn partite   5
e siàn venute a voi qui di presente:
la man che ci movea dice che sente
cose dubbiose nel core apparite;

le quali hanno destrutto sì costui
ed hannol posto sì presso a la morte,   10
ch'altro non v'è rimaso che sospiri.

Or vi preghiàn quanto possiàn più forte
che non sdegn[i]ate di tenerci noi,
tanto ch'un poco di pietà vi miri.

18

we sad, despondent quills
sorrowing scissors and knife
have written in anguish
these words you've heard

now we speak to you leaving
and coming to your presence:
the hand moving us feels
doubtful things appear in the heart

so destroying him
so taking him near death
so but to sigh

we ask how much stronger we must be
that you don't disdain us –
until you look with a little pity

19

I' prego voi che di dolor parlate
che, per vertute di nova pietate,
non disdegn[i]ate – la mia pena udire.

Davante agli occhi miei vegg'io lo core
e l'anima dolente che s'ancide,   5
    che mor d'un colpo che li diede Amore
ed in quel punto che madonna vide.
    Lo su' gentile spirito che ride,
questi è colui che mi si fa sentire,
lo qual mi dice: "E' ti convien morire."   10

Se voi sentiste come 'l cor si dole,
dentro dal vostro cor voi tremereste:
    ch'elli mi dice sì dolci parole,
che sospirando pietà chiamereste.
    E solamente voi lo 'ntendereste: 15
ch'altro cor non poria pensar né dire
quant'è 'l dolor che mi conven soffrire.

Lagrime ascendon de la mente mia,
sì tosto come questa donna sente,
    che van faccendo per li occhi una via   20
per la qual passa spirito dolente,
    ch'entra per li [occhi] miei sì debilmente
ch'oltra non puote color discovrire
che 'l 'maginar vi si possa finire.

19

i pray you who speak of suffering
for mercy's sake
don't disdain to hear of my pain

    in front of my eyes i see my suffering
heart and soul kill themselves
    dying from Love's blow
targeted where my Lady's looks
    her gentle spirit laughs
which makes me listen
to it say – you must die

    if you were to feel how my heart suffers
you'd tremble in your own:
    how she told me such sweet words
you'd sighingly call to Pity
    and only you'd understand:
that another could neither think nor speak
such is the pain i must suffer

    tears ascend from my mind
as soon as it feels this woman
    making a path from my eyes
for my suffering spirit to pass
    entering my eyes so weakly
they can't even distinguish the colors
my imagination could provide

20

O tu, che porti nelli occhi sovente
Amor tenendo tre saette in mano,
questo mio spirto che vien di lontano
ti raccomanda l'anima dolente,

la quale ha già feruta nella mente   5
di due saette l'arcier sorïano;
a la terza apre l'arco, ma sì piano
che non m'aggiunge essendoti presente:

perché saria dell'alma la salute,
che quasi giace infra le membra, morta   10
di due saette che fan tre ferute:

la prima dà piacere e disconforta,
e la seconda disia la vertute
della gran gioia che la terza porta.

20

oh you, whose eyes carry
Love holding three arrows
my spirit coming from afar
commends to you my suffering soul

already they've wounded my mind
those two arrows of the Syrian archer
the third is bowed but so softly
it doesn't arrive while i'm in your presence:

because the safety of my soul
– that nearly lies within my bones –
would die from two arrows making three wounds

the first giving pleasure and pain
the second would give the virtue
of great joy that the third carries

21

O donna mia, non vedestù colui
che 'n su lo core mi tenea la mano
quando ti rispondea fiochetto e piano
per la temenza de li colpi sui?

E' fu Amore, che, trovando noi,   5
meco ristette, che venia lontano,
in guisa d'arcier presto sorïano
acconcio sol per uccider altrui.

E' trasse poi de li occhi tuo' sospiri,
i qua' me saettò nel cor sì forte,   10
ch'i' mi partì' sbigotito fuggendo.

Allor m'aparve di sicur la Morte,
acompagnata di quelli martiri
che soglion consumare altru' piangendo.

21

o my Lady, didn't you see him
who took my hand onto his heart
when i answered you softly and weakly
full of fear from his arrows

it was Love – who finding us
with me restrained – coming from afar
in the guise of the Syrian archer
only suited to killing others

who drew sighs from your eyes
wounding me so strongly in my heart
that i fled trembling

then Death for sure appeared to me
accompanied by those tortures
that usually consume others crying

22

Veder poteste, quando v'inscontrai,
quel paüroso spirito d'amore
lo qual sòl apparir quand'om si more,
e 'n altra guisa non si vede mai.

Elli mi fu sì presso, ch'i' pensai   5
ch'ell' uccidesse lo dolente core:
allor si mise nel morto colore
l'anima trista per voler trar guai;

ma po' sostenne, quando vide uscire
degli occhi vostri un lume di merzede,   10
che porse dentr' al cor nova dolcezza;

e quel sottile spirito che vede
soccorse gli altri, che credean morire,
gravati d'angosciosa debolezza.

22

you could see when i met you
that fearsome spirit of Love
that only appears when a man dies
otherwise never

he was so close i thought
he'd kill my suffering heart:
then my sad soul – wanting to avoid trouble –
assumed Death's pallor

but it helped little when he saw
Mercy's light coming from your eyes
putting a fresh sweetness in my heart

and that graceful spirit he saw
aiding others who believed they were dying
burdened with anxious weakness

23

Io vidi li occhi dove Amor si mise
quando mi fece di sé pauroso,
che mi guardâr com'io fosse noioso:
allora dico che 'l cor si divise;

e se non fosse che la donna rise,   5
i' parlerei di tal guisa doglioso,
ch'Amor medesmo ne farei cruccioso,
che fe' lo immaginar che mi conquise.

Dal ciel si mosse un spirito, in quel punto
che quella donna mi degnò guardare,   10
e vennesi a posar nel mio pensero:

elli mi conta sì d'Amor lo vero,
che[d] ogni sua virtù veder mi pare
sì com'io fosse nello suo cor giunto.

23

i saw Love in eyes
making me so afraid
he considered me irksome
i tell you my heart splinters

if not for her smile
i would speak sufferingly
making Love himself angry
he who made the image that conquered me

a heavenly spirit came when
that Lady deigned look at me
posing this thought

he told me the truth about love
so i see her every virtue
as if i were already in her heart

24

Un amoroso sguardo spiritale
m'ha renovato Amor, tanto piacente
ch'assa' più che non sòl ora m'assale
e stringem' a pensar coralemente

della mia donna, verso cu' non vale   5
merzede né pietà né star soffrente,
ché soventora mi dà pena tale,
che 'n poca parte il mi' cor vita sente.

Ma quando sento che sì dolce sguardo
dentro degli occhi mi passò al core   10
e posevi uno spirito di gioia,

di farne a lei mercé, di ciò non tardo:
così pregata foss'ella d'Amore
ch'un poco di pietà no i fosse noia!

24

Love's amorous spiritual glance
renewed me, so pleasing
i can't handle its onslaught
forcing heartfelt thoughts

of my Lady against whom
avail not mercy, pity or suffering
because she always gives me such pain
rarely my heart feels alive

but when i feel such a sweet glance
pierce my eyes to my heart
placing a spirit of joy there

i don't wait to thank her:
were she so entreated by Love
that a little pity wouldn't annoy her!

25

Posso degli occhi miei novella dire,
la qual è tale che piace sì al core
che di dolcezza ne sospir' Amore.

    Questo novo plager che 'l meo cor sente
fu tratto sol d'una donna veduta,   *5*
    la qual è sì gentil e avenente
e tanta adorna, che 'l cor la saluta.
    Non è la sua biltate canosciuta
da gente vile, ché lo suo colore
chiama intelletto di troppo valore.   *10*

    Io veggio che negli occhi suoi risplende
una vertù d'amor tanto gentile,
    ch'ogni dolce piacer vi si comprende;
e move a loro un'anima sottile,
    respetto della quale ogn'altra è vile: *15*
e non si pò di lei giudicar fòre
altro che dir: "Quest' è novo splendore."

    Va', ballatetta, e la mia donna trova,
e tanto li domanda di merzede,
    che gli occhi di pietà verso te mova   *20*
par quei che 'n lei ha tutta la sua fede;
    e s'ella questa grazia ti concede,
mandi una voce d'allegrezza fòre,
che mostri quella che t'ha fatto onore.

25

may i tell you news of my eyes
that is so pleasing to the heart
Love moans sweetly

    this new heartfelt pleasure
extracted by a woman i saw
    so gentle, graceful and complete
my heart greeted her
    the vile know not her beauty
as her person
requires lofty intellect

    i see shining in her eyes
Love's virtue so gentle
    every sweet pleasure is understood
with a graceful soul moving to them
    in respect to it all others are crude:
so one can't judge her
but by saying – this is new splendor –

    go, little ballad, find my Lady
begging her for Mercy
    so her pitying eyes turn to you
to the faithful
    and if she consents
send out a cry of joy
that shows her it's an honor

26

Veggio negli occhi de la donna mia
un lume pien di spiriti d'amore,
che porta uno piacer novo nel core,
sì che vi desta d'allegrezza vita.

    Cosa m'aven, quand' i' le son presente,   *5*
ch'i' non la posso a lo 'ntelletto dire:
veder mi par de la sua labbia uscire
una sì bella donna, che la mente
    comprender no la può, che 'mmantenente
ne nasce un'altra di bellezza nova,   *10*
da la qual par ch'una stella si mova
e dica: "La salute tua è apparita."

    Là dove questa bella donna appare
s'ode una voce che le vèn davanti
e par che d'umiltà il su' nome canti   *15*
sì dolcemente, che, s'i' 'l vo' contare,
    sento che 'l su' valor mi fa tremare;
e movonsi nell'anima sospiri
che dicon: "Guarda; se tu coste' miri,
vedra' la sua vertù nel ciel salita."   *20*

26

i see in my Lady's eyes
a light full of the spirit of Love
that brings a new spirit to my heart
awakening there a cheerful life

    what happens to me before her
i can't explain to my intellect:
seeing in her face
such a beautiful Lady my mind
    can't understand that suddenly
another new beauty is born from it
appearing like a shooting star
saying – your salvation has appeared

    there where this beauty appears
one hears a voice proceed
singing its name – Humility –
so sweetly that i want to join
    i feel her worth make me tremble
and move sighs in my soul
that say – beware, if you look at her
your virtue will ascend to heaven

27

Donna me prega,
              per ch'eo voglio dire
d'un accidente
              che sovente
                            è fero   5
ed è sì altero
              ch'è chiamato amore:
sì chi lo nega
              possa 'l ver sentire!

Ed a presente   10
              conoscente
                            chero,
perch'io no spero
              ch'om di basso core
a tal ragione porti canoscenza: 15
     chè senza
              natural dimostramento
non ho talento
              di voler provare
là dove posa, e chi lo fa creare,   20
e qual sia sua vertute e sua potenza,
     l'essenza
              poi e ciascun suo movimento,
e 'l piacimento
              che 'l fa dire amare,   25
e s'omo per veder lo pò mostrare.

27

Woman asks me
            for which I want to speak
of something extraneous
                                    often

                                                fierce

so proud
            called love:
whoever denies it
            can hear the truth!

About this
            knowing
                                    expert
as I don't expect
            men with vile hearts
      to know:
because without
                  natural demonstration
I haven't the desire
                        the will to prove
where it rests, and who makes it act
      what are its virtues, its power
its essence
                  each movement
its predilection
                        making one call it love-ing
demonstrably seen...

In quella parte
                    dove sta memora
prende suo stato,
                    sì formato,   30
                                        come
diaffan da lume,
                    d'una scuritate
la qual da Marte
                    vène, e fa demora;   35
elli è creato
                    ed ha sensato
                                        nome,
d'alma costume
                    e di cor volontate.   40

Vèn da veduta forma che s'intende,
che prende
                    nel possibile intelletto,
come in subietto,
                    loco e dimoranza.   45
In quella parte mai non ha pesanza
perché da qualitate non descende:
     resplende
                    in sé perpetüal effetto;
non ha diletto   50
                    ma consideranza;
sì che non pote largir simiglianza.

In that part
          where memory
is
       so formed
                  like
translucence from light
                     from a shadow
    of Mars
        it came and lives
created
       judicious
                named
of a typical soul
       and a willing heart...

   It came from the visible form of one in love
it takes
        in the potential intellect
as in the subject
         position and residence...
Never physical there
   since it descends not from matter:
shining
       in its own perpetual effect
not delighting
       but reflecting
beyond all comparison...

Non è vertute,
             ma da quella vène
ch'è perfezione   55
             (ché si pone
                                         tale),
non razionale,
             ma che sente, dico;
for di salute   60
             giudicar mantene,
ché la 'ntenzione
             per ragione
                                vale:
discerne male   65
             in cui è vizio amico.
Di sua potenza segue spesso morte,
se forte
             la vertù fosse impedita,
la quale aita   70
             la contraria via:
non perché oppost' a naturale sia;
ma quanto che da buon perfetto tort'è
             per sorte,
             non pò dire om ch'aggia vita,   75
ché stabilita
             non ha segnoria.
A simil pò valer quand'om l'oblia.

L'essere è quando
             lo voler è tanto   80
ch'oltra misura
             di natura
                                torna,
poi non s'adorna
             di riposo mai.   85

It's not virtue
                but came from what
is perfectible
                (one posits

                                such)
not rational
                but feeling, I say
        beyond salvation
                within judgment
because its intention
                by natural law
                                prevails:
recognizing evil
                vice's friend...
        Death often follows its power
if strong
                virtue is impeded
that aids
                the opposite way:
not because it violates nature
        but based on how far sin is – by chance – from
"good perfection"
                I can't explain to one alive
because stability
                reigns not....
The same happens to one abstaining...

        It exists when
                        desire is
beyond measure
                        of nature
                                it comes
then does not honor
                        never resting...

Move, cangiando
        color, riso in pianto,
e la figura
    con paura
            storna;   90
poco soggiorna;
    ancor di lui vedrai
che 'n gente di valor lo più si trova.
   La nova
      qualità move sospiri,   95
e vol ch'om miri
        'n non formato loco,
destandos' ira la qual manda foco
(imaginar nol pote om che nol prova),
   né mova   100
      già però ch'a lui si tiri,
e non si giri
      per trovarvi gioco:
né cert'ha mente gran saver né poco.
De simil tragge   105
      complessione sguardo
   che fa parere
        lo piacere
           certo:
non pò coverto   110
    star, quand'è sì giunto.
  Non già selvagge
        le bieltà son dardo,
ché tal volere
    per temere   115
          è sperto:
consiegue merto
    spirito ch'è punto.

It moves, changing
      color, laughs to tears
and the victim
    with fear
                turns away
of short duration
          you'll see it
    more in people of worth...
Fresh
      it causes sighs
wanting attention
         in an ambiguous place
awakening an ire that causes fire
    (unimaginable to the inexperienced)
neither moving
        for one is already drawn
and can't escape
      to find delight
nor knowing anything certain...
    Similarly it extracts
      a glance
that appears
      pleasurable
             certain
unable to hide
     or remain once arrived...
Not initially savage
       beauties are arrows

so excess desire
      by fear
            reigns
attaining redemption
      the spirit that is wounded...

E non si pò conoscer per lo viso:
    compriso   120
           bianco in tale obietto cade;
e, chi ben aude,
           forma non si vede:
dunqu' elli meno, che da lei procede.
For di colore, d'essere diviso,   125
    assiso
           'n mezzo scuro, luce rade.
For d'ogne fraude
           dico, degno in fede,
che solo di costui nasce mercede.   130

Tu puoi sicuramente gir, canzone,
    là 've ti piace, ch'io t'ho sì adornata
    ch'assai laudata
               sarà tua ragione
da le persone   135
           c'hanno intendimento:
di star con l'altre tu non hai talento.

One's face reveals nothing:
repressed
        pallor overwhelming the victim
and, who hears well
           sees nothing:
therefore, Love leads, who from her proceeds...
    Colorless, a being divided,
sealed
        in the middle of darkness, erasing
light...Beyond deceit
                I say in good faith
mercy comes only from Love...

    go with certainty, my song
where you please, since I've so adorned you
that so praised
        will be your nature
by people
        who are in love:
you won't desire to stay with outsiders...

28

Pegli occhi fere un spirito sottile,
che fa 'n la mente spirito destare,
dal qual si move spirito d'amare,
ch'ogn'altro spiritel[lo] fa gentile.

Sentir non pò di lu' spirito vile,   5
di cotanta vertù spirito appare:
quest' è lo spiritel che fa tremare,
lo spiritel che fa la donna umìle.

E poi da questo spirito si muove
un altro dolce spirito soave,   10
che sieg[u]e un spiritello di mercede:

lo quale spiritel spiriti piove,
ché di ciascuno spirit' ha la chiave,
per forza d'uno spirito che 'l vede.

28

spirit deft wounds my eyes so
spirit mental wakes from which
spirit of loving moves so that
spirits all are ennobled

spirit vile auditorily ignored so
spirit virtuous appears
spirit same makes me tremble
spirit ditto makes women humble

spirit from which moves
spirit sweet and smooth
spirit of Mercy following

spirit such making spirits cry as
spirit said has each spirit's key by virtue of
spirit that sees it

29

Una giovane donna di Tolosa,
bell'e gentil, d'onesta leggiadria,
è tant'e dritta e simigliante cosa,
ne' suoi dolci occhi, della donna mia,

che fatt' ha dentro al cor disiderosa   5
l'anima, in guisa che da lui si svia
e vanne a lei; ma tant'è paurosa,
che non le dice di qual donna sia.

Quella la mira nel su' dolce sguardo,
ne lo qual face rallegrare Amore   10
perché v'è dentro la sua donna dritta;

po' torna, piena di sospir', nel core,
ferita a morte d'un tagliente dardo
che questa donna nel partir li gitta.

29

a young Lady of Tolosa
beautiful, noble, of virtuous grace
so perfect and resembling something
in her sweet eyes of my Lady

that she made my desiring soul in
my heart leave
and go to her – but so fearful
that it couldn't tell whose girl it was

she looked at him with that sweet gaze
that makes Love rejoice
because inside she is my Lady to a "T"

shortly it returns sighing to my heart
wounded by a piercing arrow
she threw at parting

30

Era in penser d'amor quand' i' trovai
due foresette nove.
L'una cantava: "E' piove
gioco d'amore in noi."

    Era la vista lor tanto soave   5
e tanto queta, cortese e umìle,
    ch'i' dissi lor: "Vo', portate la chiave
di ciascuna vertù alta e gentile.
    Deh, foresette, no m'abbiate a vile
per lo colpo ch'io porto;   10
questo cor mi fue morto
poi che 'n Tolosa fui."

    Elle con gli occhi lor si volser tanto
che vider come 'l cor era ferito
    e come un spiritel nato di pianto   15
era per mezzo de lo colpo uscito.
    Poi che mi vider così sbigottito,
disse l'una, che rise:
"Guarda come conquise
forza d'amor costui!"   20

    L'altra, pietosa, piena di mercede,
fatta di gioco in figura d'amore,
    disse: "'L tuo colpo, che nel cor si vede,
fu tratto d'occhi di troppo valore,
    che dentro vi lasciaro uno splendore   25
ch'i' nol posso mirare.
Dimmi se ricordare
di quegli occhi ti puoi."

30

i was deep in thoughts of Love when i found
two young country girls
one was singing – the game of Love
pours through us

    faces so sweet
calm, courtly and humble
    that i said – you bear the key
to every lofty and noble virtue
    alas, little rustics, don't condemn me
for the wound that i carry
my heart died
when i was in Tolosa

    they turned their eyes
to see how my heart was wounded
    and how a spirit born of tears
was escaping the wound
    then seeing me so terrified
one smilingly said –
    look how the
power of Love conquered him

    the other, compassionate, full of Mercy
pleasantly resembling Love
    said – the wound one sees in your heart
was made by eyes too worthy
    leaving inside a splendor
i can't bear
can you remember
those eyes

Alla dura questione e paurosa
la qual mi fece questa foresetta,   30
    i' dissi: "E' mi ricorda che 'n Tolosa
donna m'apparve, accordellata istretta,
    Amor la qual chiamava la Mandetta;
giunse sì presta e forte,
che fin dentro, a la morte,   35
mi colpîr gli occhi suoi."

    Molto cortesemente mi rispuose
quella che di me prima avëa riso.
    Disse: "La donna che nel cor ti pose
co la forza d'amor tutto 'l su' viso,   40
    dentro per li occhi ti mirò sì fiso,
ch'Amor fece apparire.
Se t'è greve 'l soffrire,
raccomàndati a lui."

    Vanne a Tolosa, ballatetta mia,   45
ed entra quetamente a la Dorata,
    ed ivi chiama che per cortesia
d'alcuna bella donna sie menata
    dinanzi a quella di cui t'ho pregata;
e s'ella ti riceve,   50
dille con voce leve:
"Per merzé vegno a voi."

to the hard and fearsome question
this country girl asked
    i said – i remember in Tolosa
a Lady appeared to me tightly corseted
    Love called her Mandetta
she came so quick and strong
inside she fatally
wounded me

    very courteously responded
the first who had laughed
    saying – the Lady who put
her face in your heart with Love's force
    looked into your eyes so forcefully
that love appeared
if he hurt you
pay homage to him

    go to Tolosa, my ballatetta,
and enter Notre-Dame de la Daurade
    and ask if by courtesy
a particular beautiful Lady is there
    it's before her i ask you to go
and if she receives you
tell her out loud –
i come to you for Mercy

31

Gli occhi di quella gentil foresetta
hanno distretta – sì la mente mia,
ch'altro non chiama che le', né disia.

   Ella mi fere sì, quando la sguardo,
ch'i' sento lo sospir tremar nel core: 5
   esce degli occhi suoi, che mè' [ne 'mb] ardo,
un gentiletto spirito d'amore,
   lo qual è pieno di tanto valore,
quando mi giunge, l'anima va via,
come colei che soffrir nol poria.   10

   I' sento pianger for li miei sospiri,
quando la mente di lei mi ragiona;
   e veggio piover per l'aere martiri
che struggon di dolor la mia persona,
   sì che ciascuna vertù m'abandona,   15
in guisa ch'i' non so là 'v'i' mi sia:
sol par che Morte m'aggia 'n sua balìa.

   Sì mi sento disfatto, che Mercede
già non ardisco nel penser chiamare,
   ch'i' trovo Amor che dice: "Ella si vede   20
tanto gentil, che non pò 'maginare
   ch'om d'esto mondo l'ardisca mirare
che non convegna lui tremare in pria;
ed i', s'i' la sguardasse, ne morria."

31

the eyes of that gentle country girl
so bound my mind
it thought of no desire but her

    so wounding me looking at her
i feel sighs tremble in my heart
    i fall in love when a gentle
spirit of love comes from her eyes
    so worthy
as it arrives, my soul flees
as one who can't suffer

    i feel tears surpass my sighs
when her mind reasons with me
    and i see torments rain through the air
destroying me with pain
    so every virtue abandons me
leaving me lost
with only Death having power over me

    feeling so undone
i dare not call Mercy
though finding Love who says – she seems so gentle
so noble i can't imagine
    any man daring to look
without trembling in her presence
even i would die if i looked –

Ballata, quando tu sarai presente   25
a gentil donna, sai che tu dirai
   de l'angoscia[to] dolorosamente?
Di': "Quelli che mi manda a voi trâ guai,
   però che dice che non spera mai
trovar Pietà di tanta cortesia,   30
ch'a la sua donna faccia compagnia."

ballad, when you reach
the noble Lady, you know you will
tell sadly of my torment
saying – he who sends me suffers
for this reason he doesn't hope
to ever find the courteous Pity
that keeps you company

32

Quando di morte mi conven trar vita
e di pesanza gioia,
come di tanta noia
lo spirito d'amor d'amar m'invita?

    Come m'invita lo meo cor d'amare,   5
lasso, ch'è pien di doglia
e di sospir' sì d'ogni parte priso,
    che quasi sol merzé non pò chiamare,
e di vertù lo spoglia
l'afanno che m'ha già quasi conquiso?   10
    Canto, piacere, beninanza e riso
me'n son dogli' e sospiri:
guardi ciascuno e miri
che Morte m'è nel viso già salita!

    Amor, che nasce di simil piacere,   15
dentro lo cor si posa
formando di disio nova persona;
    ma fa la sua virtù in vizio cadere,
sì ch'amar già non osa
qual sente come servir guiderdona.   20
    Dunque d'amar perché meco ragiona?
Credo sol perché vede
ch'io domando mercede
a Morte, ch'a ciascun dolor m'adita.

32

since when must i draw life from death
and joy from burdens
as from so much trouble
Love's spirit urges me to love

    as when he makes my heart love –
alas – so full of pain
and sighs in every corner
    it almost can't beg for Mercy
and robbed of all essence
by the anxiety that has almost conquered me
    song, pleasure, kindness, and smiles
are sorrows and sighs in me
look everyone to see
that Death is on my face

    Love, born from a like pleasure,
in my heart
forming a new person from desire
    but making his virtue fall into vice
so he doesn't dare love
she who feels like rewarding service
    why does he reason with me about loving
i believe only because he sees
that i ask for Mercy
from Death who wills me every torment

I' mi posso blasmar di gran pesanza   25
più che nessun giammai:
ché Morte d'entro 'l cor me tragge un core
    che va parlando di crudele amanza,
che ne' mie' forti guai
m'affanna là ond'i' prendo ogni valore.   30
    Quel punto maladetto, sia ch'Amore
nacque di tal manera
che la mia vita fera
li fue, di tal piacere, a lui gradita.

i can damn great suffering
as well as any
because inside my heart Death plucks out a heart
    that speaks of a cruel mistress
who in my deep troubles
afflicts my deepest essence
    cursed be that moment when Love
was born in such a way
that my savage life
was, with such pleasure, his reward

33

Io temo che la mia disaventura
non faccia sì ch'i' dica: "I' mi dispero,"
però ch'i' sento nel cor un pensero
che fa tremar la mente di paura,

e par che dica: "Amor non t'assicura   5
in guisa, che tu possi di leggero
a la tua donna sì contar il vero,
che Morte non ti ponga 'n sua figura."

De la gran doglia che l'anima sente
si parte da lo core uno sospiro   10
che va dicendo: "Spiriti, fuggite."

Allor d'un uom che sia pietoso miro,
che consolasse mia vita dolente
dicendo: "Spiritei, non vi partite!"

33

i fear from my misfortune
i can say none other than – i'm desperate –
because i feel a thought in my heart
make my mind tremble with fear

and appear to say – Love doesn't assure you
in a way that you might easily tell
the truth to your Lady
without Death invading you through her –

because of the pain my soul feels
a sorrow leaves my heart
saying – spirits flee –

then i seek a compassionate man
who would console my wretched life
saying – spirits, don't leave

34

La forte e nova mia disaventura
m'ha desfatto nel core
ogni dolce penser, ch'i' avea, d'amore.

Disfatta m'ha già tanto de la vita,
che la gentil, piacevol donna mia   5
    dall'anima destrutta s'è partita,
sì ch'i' non veggio là dov'ella sia.
Non è rimaso in me tanta balìa,
ch'io de lo su' valore
possa comprender nella mente fiore.   10

Vèn, che m'uccide, un[o] sottil pensero,
che par che dica ch'i' mai no la veggia:
    questo [è] tormento disperato e fero,
che strugg' e dole e 'ncende ed amareggia.
    Trovar non posso a cui pietate cheggia,   15
mercé di quel signore
che gira la fortuna del dolore.

    Pieno d'angoscia, in loco di paura,
lo spirito del cor dolente giace
    per la Fortuna che di me non cura,   20
c'ha volta Morte dove assai mi spiace,
    e da speranza, ch'è stata fallace,
nel tempo ch'e' si more
m'ha fatto perder dilettevole ore.

34

my latest cruel misfortune
undid in my heart
every sweet thought i had of Love

    already so undone in life
my gentle, pleasing Lady
    has left my destroyed soul
her whereabouts unknown
    not enough power left in me
so her worthiness
can flower in my mind

    a subtle thought came killing me
saying i'll never see her
    desperate and fierce
this torment destroys, hurts, burns, and embitters
    i can't find whom one asks pity
Mercy of that lord
who controls suffering's fortune

    full of anguish, in fear's alley
my suffering heart's spirit lies down
    before uncaring fortune
who's directed Death to me
    and hope – who's been false –
in Death's moment
made me lose pleasurable time

Parole mie disfatt' e paurose,   *25*
là dove piace a voi di gire andate;
    ma sempre sospirando e vergognose
lo nome de la mia donna chiamate.
    Io pur rimango in tant'aversitate
che, qual mira de fòre,   *30*
vede la Morte sotto al meo colore.

unravelled and fearful words
go where it pleases you
    but always sorrowing and ashamed
call my Lady's name
    meanwhile i'll remain in such adversity
that an outsider
will see Death under my skin

35

Perch'i' no spero di tornar giammai,
ballatetta, in Toscana,
va' tu, leggera e piana,
dritt'a la donna mia,
che per sua cortesia   5
ti farà molto onore.

    Tu porterai novelle di sospiri
piene di dogli' e di molta paura;
        ma guarda che persona non ti miri
che sia nemica di gentil natura: 10
        ché certo per la mia disaventura
tu saresti contesa,
tanto da lei ripresa
che mi sarebbe angoscia;
dopo la morte, poscia,   15
pianto e novel dolore.

    Tu senti, ballatetta, che la morte
mi stringe sì, che vita m'abbandona;
        e senti come 'l cor si sbatte forte
per quel che ciascun spirito ragiona.   20

35

because i expect never to return
to Tuscany, little ballad,
go agile and complete
to my Lady
who'll honor you
because of her courtesy

you'll carry news of sighs
filled with pain and fear
but beware the glance
from an enemy of gentle nature
because of my mishap
you will be hindered
as well as rebuked by her
who would anguish me
after death
crying and new pain

you feel, little ballad, death
squeezing me so life leaves me
and you feel as my heart fights
for what each spirit ponders

Tanto è distrutta già la mia persona,
ch'i' non posso soffrire:
se tu mi vuoi servire,
mena l'anima teco
(molto di ciò ti preco)   25
quando uscirà del core.

Deh, ballatetta mia, a la tu' amistate
quest'anima che trema raccomando:
    menala teco, nella sua pietate,
a quella bella donna a cu' ti mando.   30
    Deh, ballatetta, dille sospirando,
quando le se' presente:
"Questa vostra servente
vien per istar con voi,
partita da colui   35
che fu servo d'Amore."

Tu, voce sbigottita e deboletta
ch'esci piangendo de lo cor dolente,
    coll'anima e con questa ballatetta
va' ragionando della strutta mente.   40
    Voi troverete una donna piacente,
di sì dolce intelletto
che vi sarà diletto
starle davanti ognora.
Anim', e tu l'adora   45
sempre, nel su' valore.

so destroyed is my person
i'm unable to suffer
if you want to serve me
lead my soul
– i beg you –
when you leave my heart

alas, little ballad, i commend
my trembling soul to you
lead it in its piety
to the Lady i send you to
alas, little ballad, sigh
to her presence
– your servant
comes to stay
parted from him
who serves Love –

you, terrified and weakened voice
issuing from my sorrowing heart,
go tell of my destroyed mind
along with my soul and this little song
you will find a pleasing Lady
of such sweet intellect
you'll be pleased
to always stay before her
and my soul, you'll
always adore her worth

36

Certe mie rime a te mandar vogliendo
del greve stato che lo meo cor porta,
Amor aparve a me in figura morta
e disse: "Non mandar, ch'i' ti riprendo,

però che, se l'amico è quel ch'io 'ntendo,   5
e' non avrà già sì la mente accorta,
ch'udendo la 'ngiuliosa cosa e torta
ch'i' ti fo sostener tuttora ardendo,

ched e' non prenda sì gran smarrimento
ch'avante ch'udit' aggia tua pesanza   10
non si diparta da la vita il core.

E tu conosci ben ch'i' sono Amore;
però ti lascio questa mia sembianza
e pòrtone ciascun tu' pensamento."

36

wanting i send you certain poems
about my heart's grave state
Love appeared as a dead figure
saying – i warn you not to send them

because if the friend is who i imagine
his mind won't be ready
to hear of the injustice
i make you burn with

he won't take such a large loss
as if his heart would leave him
if he heard your ponderousness

and you well know i'm Love
for this reason i leave you my semblance
and carry away your thoughts

37A

Dante ai fedeli d'amore

A ciascun'alma presa e gentil core
nel cui cospetto ven lo dir presente,
in ciò che mi rescrivan suo parvente,
salute in lor segnor, cioè Amore.

Già eran quasi atterzate l'ore   5
del tempo che onne stella n'è lucente,
quando m'apparve Amor subitamente,
cui essenza membrar mi dà orrore.

Allegro mi sembrava Amor tenendo
meo core in mano, e ne le braccia avea   10
madonna involta in un drappo dormendo.

Poi la svegliava, e d'esto core ardendo
lei paventosa umilmente pascea:
appresso gir lo ne vedea piangendo.

37A

Dante to Love's Faithful

to each captive and nobly gentle heart
in whose sight comes this present poem
returning to me his response
of greeting to their Lord, that is, Love

already it was four am
at that time when every star shines
when Love suddenly appeared to me
whose essential form gives me horror to
remember

happily Love seemed to hold
my heart in his hand and in his arm
had my Lady wrapped in a mantle sleeping

then he woke her and this burning heart
to fearful her humbly fed:
then i saw him turn away crying

37B

Vedeste, al mio parere, onne valore
e tutto gioco e quanto bene om sente,
se foste in prova del segnor valente
che segnoreggia il mondo de l'onore,

poi vive in parte dove noia more,   5
e tien ragion nel cassar de la mente;
sì va soave per sonno a la gente,
che 'l cor ne porta senza far dolore.

Di voi lo core ne portò, veggendo
che vostra donna la morte chedea: 10
nodriala dello cor, di ciò temendo.

Quando v'apparve che se 'n gia dolendo,
fu 'l dolce sonno ch'allor si compiea,
ché 'l su' contraro lo venìa vincendo.

37B

if it were mine, you'd see every value
and joy and good feeling
if you knew of the worthy lord
who rules the world of honor

living where trouble dies
reasoning in the mind's citadel
visiting people's dreams
painlessly transporting their hearts

he took your heart away seeing
your Lady ask for your death
nourishing her with your trembling heart

when you see him leave sorrowing
the sweet trance ends
defeated by its enemy

38A

Dante a Guido Cavalcanti

Guido, i' vorrei che tu e Lapo ed io
fossimo presi per incantamento
e messi in un vasel, ch'ad ogni vento
per mare andasse al voler vostro e mio;

sì che fortuna od altro tempo rio   5
non ci potesse dare impedimento,
anzi, vivendo sempre in un talento,
di stare insieme crescesse 'l disio.

E monna Vanna e monna Lagia poi
con quella ch'è sul numer de le trenta   10
con noi ponesse il buono incantatore:

e quivi ragionar sempre d'amore
e ciascuna di lor fosse contenta,
sì come i' credo che saremmo noi.

38A

Dante to Guido Cavalcanti

Guido, i would like that you and Lapo and i
    would be taken by enchantment
        and placed in a vessel so any wind
            at sea would move to your and my will

    so that storms or other bad weather
    could not hinder us
        rather always living in hope
        of staying together to increase the desire

and Lady Vanna and Lady Lagia then
    with her on number thirty
        would place the good sorcerer with us

        and there always inquiring about Love
        every one of them would be as content
            as – i believe – would we

38B

S'io fosse quelli che d'amor fu degno,
del qual non trovo sol che rimembranza,
e la donna tenesse altra sembianza,
assai mi piaceria siffatto legno.

E tu, che se' de l'amoroso regno   5
là onde di merzé nasce speranza,
riguarda se 'l mi' spirito ha pesanza:
ch'un prest' arcier di lui ha fatto segno

e tragge l'arco, che li tese Amore,
sì lietamente, che la sua persona   10
par che di gioco porti signoria.

Or odi maraviglia ch'el disia:
lo spirito fedito li perdona,
vedendo che li strugge il suo valore.

38B

if i were one worthy of Love
not finding other than memories
and the Lady changing her mind
such a boat would please me

and you, of the amorous realm
where hope is born of mercy,
would consider if my spirit is troubled
targeted by an archer who

draws the bow held by Love
so happily that he
would seem to reign over play

now hear the marvel he desires:
my wounded spirit forgives
even seeing Love destroy him

39

Se vedi Amore, assai ti priego, Dante,
in parte là 've Lapo sia presente,
che non ti gravi di por sì la mente
che mi riscrivi s'elli 'l chiama amante

e se la donna li sembla avenante,   5
ch'e' si le mostra vinto fortemente:
ché molte fiate così fatta gente
suol per gravezza d'amor far sembiante.

Tu sai che ne la corte là 'v'e regna
e' non vi può servir om che sia vile   10
a donna che là entro sia renduta:

se la sofrenza lo servente aiuta,
può di leggier cognoscer nostro sire,
lo quale porta di merzede insegna.

39

if you see Love, Dante,
in Lapo's presence
don't burden your mind
by writing me if he's called a lover

and if women grace him
so he shows himself to them defeated
because many people waste their breath
on false love

you know that in her court she reigns
and a vile man can't serve
a woman seated there

if suffering aids the servant
quickly he may know our lord
who carries Mercy's banner

40

Dante, un sospiro messagger del core
subitamente m'assalì dormendo,
ed io mi disvegliai allor, temendo
ched e' non fosse in compagnia d'Amore.

Po' mi girai, e vidi 'l servitore   5
di monna Lagia che venìa dicendo:
"Aiutami, Pietà!" sì che piangendo
i' presi di merzé tanto valore,

ch'i' giunsi Amore ch'affilava i dardi.
Allor l'adomandai del su' tormento,   10
ed elli mi rispuose in questa guisa:

"Di' al servente che la donna è prisa,
e tengola per far su' piacimento;
e se no 'l crede, di' ch'a li occhi guardi."

40

Dante, a sighing messenger of the heart
assailed me suddenly in my dreams
that i uprooted myself fearing
he was in Love's company

then i turned seeing Lady Laggia's
servant who came saying –
help me, Pity! – crying
i drew strength from Mercy

because i found Love sharpening arrows
then i asked him of her torment
and he told me –

tell her servant that his Lady is taken
and kept for her own pleasure
and if he's skeptical, tell him to look in her eyes –

41

I' vegno 'l giorno a te 'nfinite volte
e trovoti pensar troppo vilmente:
molto mi dòl della gentil tua mente
e d'assai tue vertù che ti son tolte.

Solevanti spiacer persone molte;   5
tuttor fuggivi l'annoiosa gente;
di me parlavi sì coralemente,
che tutte le tue rime avie ricolte.

Or non ardisco, per la vil tua vita,
far mostramento che tu' dir mi piaccia,   10
né 'n guisa vegno a te, che tu mi veggi.

Se 'l presente sonetto spesso leggi,
lo spirito noioso che ti caccia
si partirà da l'anima invilita.

41

each day i come to you an infinity of times
finding you with base thoughts
i mourn the loss of your noble mind
and your many virtues

the many often displeased you
you've always fled the tedious
you've spoken warmly of me
so i've gathered all your poems

now i publicly dare neither to praise your song
because of your vile life
nor even approach you

if you often read my sonnet
the troublesome spirit haunting you
will leave your disheartened soul

42

Certo non è de lo 'ntelletto acolto
quel che staman ti fece disonesto:
or come già, ['n] men [che non] dico, presto
t'aparve rosso spirito nel volto?

Sarebbe forse che t'avesse sciolto   5
Amor da quella ch'è nel tondo sesto?
o che vil razzo t'avesse richesto
a por te lieto ov' i' son tristo molto?

Di te mi dole: di me guata quanto
che me 'n fiede la mia donna 'n traverso,   10
tagliando ciò ch'Amor porta soave!

Ancor dinanzi m'è rotta la chiave
del su' disdegno che nel mi' cor verso,
sì che n'ho l'ira, e d'allegrezza è pianto.

42

surely it wasn't your cultured mind
that made you lie to me this morning
about what happened – dare i say – suddenly
you seem embarrassed

perhaps Love dissolved you
from her in the sixth circle
or some vile force made
you happy and me sad

i worry about you – look at how
i hurt myself by crossing my Lady
cheating Love's sweet gift

even now before my eyes the key
of her disdain twists in my heart
so that i get angry and joy turns to tears

43

Gianni, quel Guido salute
ne la tua bella e dolce salute.
Significàstimi, in un sonetto
rimatetto,
il voler de la giovane donna   5
che ti dice: "Fa' di me
quel che t'è
riposo." E però ecco me
apparecchiato,
sobarcolato,   10
e d'Andrea coll'arco in mano,
e·ccogli strali e·cco' moschetti.
Guarda dove ti metti!
ché la Chiesa di Dio
sì vuole di giustizia fio.   15

43

Gianni, Guido greets
your beautiful and sweet greeting
you let me know in sonnet
rhymed
the desire of a young woman
who tells you – do with me
what you
will – and here i am
dressed
ready
with Andrew's bow in hand
along with darts and arrows
watch where you aim them
because God's Church
will want an arm and a leg in judgment

44A

Bernardo da Bologna
a Guido Cavalcanti

A quella amorosetta foresella
passò sì 'l core la vostra salute,
che sfigurìo di sue belle parute:
dond' i' l'adomanda': "Perché, Pinella?

Udistù mai di quel Guido novella?"   5
"Sì feci, ta' ch'appena l'ho credute
che s'allegaron le mortai ferute
d'amor e di su' fermamento stella,

con pura luce che spande soave.
Ma dimmi, amico, se te piace: come   10
la conoscenza di me da te l'ave?

Sì tosto com' i' 'l vidi seppe 'l nome!
Ben è, così con' si dice, la chiave.
A lui ne mandi trentamilia some."

44A

Bernardo da Bologna
to Guido Cavalcanti

inside that loving country girl
your being pierced her heart
disfiguring her beautiful looks
so i asked her – why Pinella

did you listen to young Guido –
because he made me believe him
closing the mortal wounds
of Love and the stars

with pure light sweetly overflowing
but tell me, friend, how
you found out about this

when it was over, i knew his type
actions – so to speak – are louder than words
send him a ton

44B

Guido Cavalcanti
al detto Bernardo risponde

Ciascuna fresca e dolce fontanella
prende in Liscian[o] chiarezz' e vertute,
Bernardo amico mio, solo da quella
che ti rispuose a le tue rime agute:

però che, in quella parte ove favella   *5*
Amor delle bellezze c'ha vedute,
dice che questa gentiletta e bella
tutte nove adornezze ha in sé compiute.

Avegna che la doglia i' porti grave
per lo sospiro, ché di me fa lume   *10*
lo core ardendo in la disfatta nave,

mand' io a la Pinella un grande fiume
pieno di lammie, servito da schiave
bell' e adorn' e di gentil costume.

44B

Guido Cavalcanti
responds to Bernardo

each fresh and sweet source
is clear and strong in Lisciano,
Bernard my friend, aside from that one
who responds to your pointed poems

for that reason – in that place where
Love tells of experienced beauties –
he says that this noble beauty is
freshly complete and perfect

although i bear great pain
for her sorrows because such enlightenment makes
my burning heart an overturned vessel

send Pinella a great stream
of nymphs served by slaves
beautiful and complete and noble

45

Se non ti caggia la tua santalena
giù per lo cólto tra le dure zolle
e vegna a man[o] d'un forese folle
che la stropicci e rèndalati a pena:

dimmi se 'l frutto che la terra mena   5
nasce di secco, di caldo o di molle;
e qual è 'l vento che l'annarca e tolle;
e di che nebbia la tempesta è piena;

e se ti piace quando la mattina
odi la boce del lavoratore   10
e 'l tramazzare della sua famiglia.

I' ho per certo che, se la Bettina
porta soave spirito nel core,
del novo acquisto spesso ti ripiglia.

45

may you not drop your little jewel
between the plowed clumps
so it is picked up by a farmer
who fondles and keeps it

tell me if the earth's fruit
is born from dryness, heat, or moisture
and which wind blows it
and what fog fills the storm

and if you like the morning
that hears the workman's voice
and family cacophony

i certainly know that if Bettina's
heart has a sweet spirit
you'll get rid of your young acquisition

46

In un boschetto trova' pasturella
più che la stella – bella, al mi' parere.

    Cavelli avea biondetti e ricciutelli,
e gli occhi pien' d'amor, cera rosata;
      con sua verghetta pasturav' agnelli;   *5*
[di]scalza, di rugiada era bagnata;
      cantava come fosse 'namorata:
er' adornata – di tutto piacere.

    D'amor la saluta' imantenente
e domandai s'avesse compagnia;   *10*
      ed ella mi rispose dolzemente
che sola sola per lo bosco gia,
      e disse: "Sacci, quando l'augel pia,
allor disïa – 'l me' cor drudo avere."

    Po' che mi disse di sua condizione   *15*
e per lo bosco augelli audìo cantare,
      fra me stesso diss' i': "Or è stagione
di questa pasturella gio' pigliare."
    Merzé le chiesi sol che di basciare
ed abracciar, – se le fosse 'n volere.   *20*

    Per man mi prese, d'amorosa voglia,
e disse che donato m'avea 'l core;
      menòmmi sott' una freschetta foglia,
là dov'i' vidi fior' d'ogni colore;
      e tanto vi sentìo gioia e dolzore,   *25*
che 'l die d'amore – mi parea vedere.

46

i found a shepherdess in a grove
more beautiful than the stars

    honey-colored, curly hair
a blush and eyes full of love
    with her staff she tended sheep
barefoot and dew covered
    she sang as if in love
so complete with every pleasure

    i quickly greeted her with love
and asked if she had company
    and she responded so sweetly
that so alone was she
    saying – do you know, when the bird sings
it's burning, my heart is in love –

    after she told me of her condition
and i heard birds sing in the forest
    i said to myself – now is the time
to take this young thing –
    and i only asked her to kiss
and hug – if she wanted

    she took me by the hand
saying she had given me her heart
    leading me under a bush
where i saw a starburst of flowers
    and felt such joy and pain
that i thought i saw the God of Love

47

Da più a uno face un sollegismo:
in maggiore e in minor mezzo si pone,
che pruova necessario sanza rismo;
da ciò ti parti forse di ragione?

Nel profferer, che cade 'n barbarismo,   5
difetto di saver ti dà cagione;
e come far poteresti un sofismo
per silabate carte, fra Guittone?

Per te non fu giammai una figura;
non fòri ha posto il tuo un argomento;   10
induri quanto più disci; e pon' cura,

ché 'ntes' ho che compon' d'insegnamento
volume: e fòr principio ha da natura.
Fa' ch'om non rida il tuo proponimento!

47

a syllogism makes one from many
between a major and minor one puts a middle
that proves by necessity without rhyme
do you stop this for a reason?

in the uttering that falls into barbarism
faulty knowledge gives you the reason
so how could you make a sophism
out of poetry, Fra Guittone?

for you reality never existed
your subject never goes beyond itself
the more you say, the more you confuse – so take care

because i've asked about your solid
teaching – by nature beyond principle
beware that people don't laugh at your goals

48A

A Guido Orlandi

Una figura della Donna mia
s'adora, Guido, a San Michele in Orto,
che, di bella sembianza, onesta e pia,
de' peccatori è gran rifugio e porto.

E qual con devozion lei s'umilìa,   5
chi più languisce, più n'ha di conforto:
li 'nfermi sana e' domon' caccia via
e gli occhi orbati fa vedere scorto.

Sana 'n publico loco gran langori;
con reverenza la gente la 'nchina;   10
d[i] luminara l'adornan di fòri.

La voce va per lontane camina,
ma dicon ch'è idolatra i Fra' Minori,
per invidia che non è lor vicina.

48A

To Guido Orlandi

a figure of my Lady
is worshiped in San Michele in Orto, Guido,
honest and pure and beautiful
a port of refuge for sinners

and he who worships her
failing most finds more comfort
healing the infirm and chasing away demons
clearing blind eyes

in public she cures the very ill
of those who kneel before her
as she graces sunlit streets

word of her has travelled far
but the Friars Minor say it's idolatry
out of jealousy she's not near

48B

Guido Orlandi
a Guido Cavalcanti

S'avessi detto, amico, di Maria
gratïa plena et pia:
"Rosa vermiglia se', piantata in orto,"
avresti scritta dritta simiglìa.
Et veritas et via: 5
del nostro Sire fu magione, e porto

della nostra salute, quella dia
che prese Sua contia,
[che] l'angelo le porse il suo conforto;
e certo son, chi ver' lei s'umilìa   10
e sua colpa grandia,
che sano e salvo il fa, vivo di morto.

Ahi, qual conorto − ti darò? che plori
con Deo li tuo' fallori,
e non l'altrui: le tue parti diclina,   15
e prendine dottrina
dal publican che dolse i suo' dolori.

Li Fra' Minori − sanno la divina
[i]scrittura latina,
e de la fede son difenditori   20
li bon' Predicatori:
lor predicanza è nostra medicina.

48B

Guido Orlandi
to Guido Cavalcanti

if, my friend, you would have said of Mary so
gratia plena et pia —
you are a red rose planted in an orchard —
you would have hit the mark
Et veritas et via
she was the vessel of Our Lord and the haven

of our salvation from the day
she knew of him
when the angel came before her
and i'm certain that he who kneels before her
in his great sin
will be made safe and sound, revived from the dead

ah, how should i urge you to weep of
your sins before God
and not others — to decline your grammar
and learn doctrine
from the publican who has suffered over his sins

the Fra' Minori know the divine
scriptural clarity
and the good Preachers
are defenders of the faith
their sermons are our salvation

49A

Guido Cavalcanti
a Guido Orlandi

La bella donna dove Amor si mostra,
ch'è tanto di valor pieno ed adorno,
tragge lo cor della persona vostra:
e' prende vita in far co·llei soggiorno,

perc' ha sì dolce guardia la sua chiostra,   5
che 'l sente in India ciascun lunicorno,
e la vertude l'arma a fera giostra;
vizio pos' dir no i fa crudel ritorno,

ch'ell' è per certo di sì gran valenza,
che già non manca i·llei cosa da bene,   10
ma' che Natura la creò mortale.

Poi mostra che 'n ciò mise provedenza:
ch'al vostro intendimento si convene
far, per conoscer, quel ch'a lu' sia tale.

49A

Guido Cavalcanti
to Guido Orlandi

the beautiful Lady where Love shows himself
so full and complete with value
draws your heart from you
it lives away with her

for her cloister has such a sweet defense
that each unicorn in india feels it
and virtue arms it for fierce jousting
evil – might i say? – can't return

since she is certainly of such great worth
she lacks nothing good
save for nature making her mortal

for nature shows its foresight
in order to know your heart's intended
you must do his will

49B

Risposta di Guido Orlandi
a Guido Cavalcanti

A suon di trombe, anzi che di corno,
vorria di fin' amor far una mostra
d'armati cavalier, di pasqua un giorno,
e navicare senza tiro d'ostra

ver' la Gioiosa Garda, girle intorno   5
a sua difensa, non cherendo giostra
a te, che se' di gentilezza adorno,
dicendo il ver: per ch'io la Donna nostra

di su ne prego con gran reverenza
per quella di cui spesso mi sovene,   10
ch'a lo su' sire sempre stea leale,

servando in sé l'onor, come s'avene.
Viva con Deo che ne sostene ed ale,
né mai da Lui non faccia dipartenza.

49B

Response of Guido Orlandi
to Guido Cavalcanti

to the sound of trumpets rather than horns
i would like to make an example of noble love
of armed cavaliers and a festive day
sailing without the south wind

to the Castle of Arthur's Guard around its
defenses not looking for a joust
with you adorned with gentility
speaking the truth – for i pray to Our

Lady above with reverence
whom i often remember
as loyal to her Lord

preserving her honor as it suits her –
live with God who sustains and nurtures you
never leaving him

50A

Di vil matera mi conven parlare
[e] perder rime, silabe e sonetto,
sì ch'a me ste[sso] giuro ed imprometto
a tal voler per modo legge dare.

Perché sacciate balestra legare   5
e coglier con isquadra archile in tetto
e certe fiate aggiate Ovidio letto
e trar quadrelli e false rime usare,

non pò venire per la vostra mente
là dove insegna Amor, sottile e piano,   10
di sua manera dire e di su' stato.

Già non è cosa che si porti in mano:
qual che voi siate, egli è d'un'altra gente:
sol al parlar si vede chi v'è stato.

Già non vi toccò lo sonetto primo: 15
Amore ha fabricato ciò ch'io limo.

50A

of foul matters i must speak
forgetting rhyme, syllables and the sonnet
swearing and promising to myself
to give some order to such a wish

because you can string a crossbow
and hit a target at right angles
and have read a few breaths of Ovid
and throw darts and false rhymes

it doesn't follow that your mind
can speak of Love – subtle and soft –
his manner and being

it's not something you can hold in your hand
whoever you are, he's another type
only one's speech reveals who has been there

the first sonnet did not touch you
Love has made what i'm polishing

5OB

Guido Orlandi
a Guido Cavalcanti

Amico, i' saccio ben che sa' limare
con punta lata maglia di coretto,
di palo in frasca come uccel volare,
con grande ingegno gir per loco stretto,

e largamente prendere e donare,   5
salvar lo guadagnato (ciò m'è detto),
accoglier gente, terra guadagnare.
In te non trovo, mai ch'uno difetto:

che vai dicendo intra la savia gente
faresti Amore piangere in tuo stato.   10
Non credo, poi non vede: quest'è piano.

E ben di' 'l ver, che non si porta in mano,
anzi per passïon punge la mente
dell'omo ch'ama e non si trova amato.

Io per lung' uso disusai lo primo   15
amor carnale: non tangio nel limo.

50B

Guido Orlandi
to Guido Cavalcanti

friend, i well know that you know how to polish
the chainmail of armor with a broadened point
to flit from one argument to another like a bird
to go through a tight spot with a large contraption

and generously take and give
saving the earnings (so i'm told)
gathering people and gaining ground
in you i find only one fault

you go among cultured people saying
you would make love cry over your condition
i don't believe it since love is blind – this is clear

it's better to tell the truth which can't be held in one's
        hand
rather by torment it stings the mind
of one who loves and isn't loved

from long experience i discontinued the first
carnal love – i don't touch the mud

GUIDO CAVALCANTI

51

Guata, Manetto, quella scrignutuzza,
e pon' ben mente com'è divisata
e com'è drittamente sfigurata
e quel che pare quand' ella s'agruzza!

Or, s'ella fosse vestita d'un'uzza   5
con cappellin' e di vel soggolata
ed apparisse di dìe accompagnata
d'alcuna bella donna gentiluzza,

tu non avresti niquità sì forte
né saresti angoscioso sì d'amore   10
né sì involto di malinconia,

che tu non fossi a rischio de la morte
di tanto rider che farebbe 'l core:
o tu morresti, o fuggiresti via.

51

check out the humpback, Manny
get it in your head
how she's spazzed out
and how she looks shrugging those shoulders

yo – if she were decked out
with nice threads
and was walking with
some dish

you wouldn't be so ticked
off, freaked and bummed out
about love

that you'd want to die
laughing so hard:
you'd either die or split

52

Novelle ti so dire, odi, Nerone:
che' Bondelmonti trieman di paura,
e tutti Fiorentin' no li assicura,
udendo dir che tu ha' cuor di leone:

e' più trieman di te che d'un dragone,   5
veggendo la tua faccia, ch'è sì dura
che no la riterria ponte né mura,
se non la tomba del re Pharaone.

Deh, con' tu fai grandissimo peccato:
sì alto sangue voler discacciare,   10
che tutti vanno via sanza ritegno!

Ma ben è ver che ti largâr lo pegno
di che pot[e]rai l'anima salvare:
sì fosti paziente del mercato!

52

i have news to tell you, do you hear, Nerone:
the Bondelmonti are trembling with fear
and all the Florentines don't reassure them
hearing that you have the heart of a lion

more fearful of you than of a dragon
seeing your face so hard
that no bridge or wall could rival it
except for the tomb of the Pharaoh

alas what a great sin you commit
wanting to chase out such noble blood
that all go off without control

but it is true that they forgave your debt
so you might save your soul
if you can stand the exchange

NOTES TO THE POEMS

The following notes are based primarily on Contini's notes for Cavalcanti in volume 2 of *Poeti del Duecento* and Ciccuto's commentary in Guido Cavalcanti, *Le rime.* See above, p. xlii n. 1.

Poem 1
This ballad is one of Cavalcanti's first compositions. It has a *fronte* of ABBA, BAAB and a *sirima* identical with the *ripresa*, CDDE(E)X. Notice the Provençal technique of the *coblas capfinidas,* namely the repetition of a word in the first line of each new *fronte* from the concluding line of the preceding one.

Line 1: *Fresca rosa novella* (literally "fresh new rose") recalls the first stanza of "Rosa fresca aulentissima" of the Sicilian poet, Cielo d'Alcamo. See Bruno Panvini, *Le rime della scuola siciliana,* 1:169.

Line 11: *latino* is used by Percivalle Doria from the Sicilian school as a metaphor for language or song. See Contini, 1:162.

Line 29: *adorna* is a truncated version (without suffix) in Tuscan dialect of *adornata.* See Wilhelm Meyer-Luebke, *Grammatica storica della lingua italiana e dei dialetti toscani* (Turin: Giovani Chiantore, 1931), p. 203; and Gerhard Rohlfs, *Grammatica storica della lingua italiana e dei suoi dialetti,* trans. T. Franceschi (Turin: Einaudi, 1968), 2:375-77.

I have translated *adornata* and most of its variations as "complete" instead of "adorned," perhaps an awkward word to modern ears. Moreover, Dante in *De Vulgari Eloquentia* (II, 1) points out that "a writer should adorn his verses to the best of his ability" but cautions that "adornment is the addition of something congruous." In this sense, things cannot be adorned until they are complete – i.e., harmonious or decorous.

Poem 2
This early sonnet is in Guido Guinizelli's tradition of equating one's lady with the beauty of nature. See Contini, 2:472.

Poem 3
In this type of sonnet, the poet makes the point that his lady's beauty and virtue far transcend all other beautiful things. Notice how Cavalcanti compresses his long list of treasures into one fourteen-line sentence! The composition of this sonnet resembles

Giacomo da Lentini's "Diamante né smiraldo né zafino." See
Panvini, 1:59.
Line 3: *ragionar d'amore* could also mean "conversations on
love." See note for Poem 38A, Line 12.

Poem 4

In this sonnet, the Lady appears as a transcendental being that no
earthly mortal can even begin to comprehend. Contini (2:495) sees a
progression in these first four poems of Cavalcanti. In Poems 1 and
2, the Lady's beauty is equated with all of nature. In Poem 3, she is
described as transcending all other beautiful objects. Finally, in
Poem 4 no earthly being can comprehend her by normal sensory
means. In "Io voglio del ver la mia donna laudare" (Contini, 2:
472), Guinizelli concludes that with such a Lady, "Null'om po mal
pensar fin che la vede" ("No man may think vilely seeing her").
Further along the lines of such "curative" powers, *salute* (line 13)
connotes "salvation" as well as "health." In addition, "revelation" is
implied, an indication of the Lady's transcendence of earthly
matters into the spiritual realm.

Poem 5

Cavalcanti begins to establish his poetic independence with this
sonnet. He introduces his personifications *sospiri* (sighs) and *dolor*
(suffering). The courtly tradition of the earlier poems gives way to
Cavalcanti's exploration of the nature of relationships. Here, the
Lady renders her wooer capable of no activity other than wishing for
death.
Line 3: the first clause reads literally "without those [eyes] of
you"; i.e., "without your having seen me," or "without your knowing
of my condition."
Line 10: *gente* is a Provençalism that means "nobles."

Poem 6

In this sonnet, Cavalcanti uses *spiriti* (spirits) for the first time.
Ciccuto (p. 79) explains this term of scholastic origin as the device
that connects the mind to the bodily senses and hence, the external
world. In particular for the poet, spirits allow him to know the
external world and write poetry about it.
Lines 13-14: *ella* refers to *l'alma trista.* Even though it is the
feminine pronoun, I have translated it as "he" because it is
Cavalcanti's own spirits who are asked to speak of his *alma trista.*

Poem 7

The rhyme scheme of this sonnet is unusual: ABBB BAAA CDD DCC. Contini (2:498) observes that the asymmetry of the quatrains formally reinforces the content – the turmoil and perturbations of the soul, especially in the equation (lines 3-4) of *Amore – ella more* (the state of love equals the death of the soul). At this point, Cavalcanti is no longer narrating the events of love, but discussing it as a process.

Poem 8

In this sonnet, the psychophysiology of the wooer collapses. His eyes see his beloved, and his soul flees because his moaning heart is wounded.

Line 5: ambiguity of the Provençal *trobar clus,* a poem that is deliberately ambiguous. *Amor, che...sente* can translate literally as "Love, who feels your great worth," or "Love, that your great worth feels." Cavalcanti's work is replete with this technique. See note to Poem 27 for further explanation.

Line 12: Nelson (p. 11) translates as "That can walk only by artifice." However, the verb *condurre* also means "to result in," so that I translate the sense of the line as Cavalcanti "coming to a state solely by someone's skill or mastery." The mastery is, of course, that of the Lady.

Line 14: I have translated *com' egli è morto* (as he who is dead) as "active mortality."

Poem 9

This *canzone* has a *fronte* of ABBC BAAC and a *sirima* of DeD FeF. It contains all of Guido's early observations on love: Love pronouncing a death sentence, the fleeing of one's spirits, the ineffability of love, the suffering of the wooer, and his request for salvation.

Line 22: literally, "before the great value that is demonstrated in her." *i·llei* is dialect for *in lei.* Meyer-Luebke explains that in Tuscan, the indirect object form of *Ella* (she) is *[il]laei.* For the etymology, see his *Grammatica storica,* p. 160; and Rohlfs, *Grammatica storica,* 2:136-37. Further, *dimostro* is a dialectical truncated version (without suffix) of *dimostrato.* See Meyer-Luebke, p. 203; Rohlfs, 2:375-77.

Line 30: *gentil core* is a term common to the *stilnovisti.* Dante uses it in the first line of the first poem in *La Vita Nuova:* "A ciasun'alma presa e gentil core" (To each captive and nobly gentle heart) (See Poem 37A).

Poem 10

This *ballata grande* has two *piedi* of AB, a *sirima* of BXXY, and a *ripresa* with two internal rhymes, Z(W)XX(W)Y.

Poem 11

Independent stanzas with a *fronte* of ABBC ABBC and a *sirima* of DEeFfGg, with the D the only unrhymed verse.

Line 4: *valore* can mean "power" but in a valued, good sense. Depending on the context, the connotation could be "value" as something of worth or "virtue" as something with moral goodness and right action.

Poem 12

Here the poet laments that he was not blind in order to avoid seeing his irrepressible lady.

Line 14: Contini (2:505) says that this image of the heart held in a hand might have inspired the concluding *sestina* of Dante's sonnet "A ciascun'alma presa" (Sonnet 37A).

Poem 13

In this sonnet, Cavalcanti shows the destructive force of Love as it pierces his eyes to his heart, with all of his spirits but one fleeing. An arrow comes from his Lady's eyes, striking his left side, terrifying his soul, and killing his heart.

Poem 14

In these independent stanzas the rhyme scheme is A(a)B(b)C(c)d for the *fronte* and EffgG for the *sirima*.

Line 11: Contini and Ciccuto both interpret *piova* (literally, "rains") as a metaphor for "falling" or "descending." It is a favorite verb of Cavalcanti. See Poems 17, 28, 30, and 31. "Raining" also carries the sense of "pouring," an uncontrolled emotional gush or rush that overwhelms.

Poem 15

Line 5: *angosciosi dilett[i]* (literally, "anguished pleasures) is a typical oxymoron of love poetry that expresses both the pain and joy of love. The double-edged quality of love as giver of both pleasure and suffering becomes a common conceit for Petrarch and Petrarchism; see Leonard Forster, *The Icy Fire* (Cambridge: Cambridge University Press, 1969), ch 1.

For those who feel that such strictures limit creativity, consider such varieties in the nineteenth century: Verdi's Alfredo in *La*

Traviata (Act 1) sings "Ah! Ah! croce delizia al cor" (Ah! sweet burden in my heart). See also Baudelaire's "Hymne a la beauté" from "Spleen et Idéal" in his *Les Fleurs du Mal* [an oxymoron]. Charles Baudelaire, *Selected Poems,* trans. by Joanna Richardson (London: Penguin Books, 1986), pp. 56-57. See note to Poem 32, Line 3, for further discussion.

Poem 16
  Here we see the cruel woman who deliberately destroys her lover by withholding her love.

Poem 17
  Line 3: *sconoscente* means rude or impolite, but it also connotes the opposite of its root, *conoscente* (knowing): unknowing or ignorant of the philosophy of the *stil nuovo* – a base person.

Poem 18
  Cavalcanti uses his contemporary writing implements as a metaphor for poetic creation: scissors for cutting the quills and knives for sharpening them. This action analogizes the forming of words into poems. Of course, as in all things with our melancholy poet, this relationship is not going well either.
  Note that the "iàn" verb endings are apocopated Tuscan dialect for "iamo." See Rohlfs, 2:332.

Poem 19
  This *ballata mezzana* has *stanza* of Ab, a *sirima* of BXXX and a *ripresa* of YY(y)X.

Poem 20
  According to Ovidian tradition, Love holds two arrows: the gold inspires love and the lead hate. In this case, Cavalcanti uses a third arrow that frees one from passion.
  Line 6: Contini (2:514) explains that during the Renaissance, Syrian or Damascan archers possessed legendary skill.

Poem 21
  Another poem using the theme of Love as an archer.
  Line 1: *vedestù* is *vedesti tu* with the pronoun in an enclitic position; *colui* refers to *Amore.* See Rohlfs, 2:148.
  Lines 9-10: the eye's wounding glance is equated with Love's arrows.

Poem 22

In this sonnet, Cavalcanti addresses the curative powers of the Lady.

Line 7: one of the few verses in Cavalcanti that actually describes the physical appearance of the stricken lover. *Morto colore* translates literally as "dead color" or "lifeless complexion."

Line 13: *soccorse gli altri* translates literally as "[the spirit of vision] aids others." *Altri* connotes those on the outside, not in the know. Cavalcanti's constant emphasis on the knowledge of the lover underscores that his creative enterprise dealing with love is itself an investigation.

Poem 23

The smile of the Lady has curative powers.

Poem 24

Cavalcanti's use of enjambment in this sonnet is a testimony to his poetic mastery.

Poem 25

This *ballata mezzana* has two *piedi* in each stanza of AB and a *sirima* and *ripresa* of BXX.

Poem 26

This *ballata grande* has a *fronte* of ABBA and a *sirima* and *ripresa* of ACCX.

Poem 27

This elaborate *canzone* has *strofe* of two *piedi* of (a)B(c)(c)D (d)E, a *sirima* divided into two *volte* of F(f) G(g)HH, and a *congedo* of FG(g)F(f)HH.

In deciphering this poem, no one should neglect the extremely helpful in-depth discussion by Bruno Nardi, *Dante e la cultura medievale,* chs. 1-3. Ciccuto (p. 116) refers to this poem as the doctrinal *canzone* of Cavalcanti, which expresses not only his Averroism but also serves as a manifesto for the *stilnovisti*.

Maurice Valency discusses this poem as an example that is "couched in the style of the *trobar clus* and further obfuscated by the rigors of a complex rhyme-pattern and a technical terminology" (*In Praise,* p. 228). The *trobar clus* was a complex and enigmatic poetic style developed by the Provençal troubadours. Of the *trobar clus* Valency explains: "Difficulty remained the writer's central preoccupation, but the burden was shifted. The poem was not difficult to write; it is difficult to read....Often enough, the words are clear. We simply cannot decide what they mean. The best of the *trobar clus* is characterized by a parabolic quality, the result of a studied ambiguity which implies a reserve of meaning beyond the comprehension of average intelligence" (*In Praise*, p. 125). It should be noted that the *trobar clus* is distinguished from the *trobar clar* or *leu* (a simple and clear poem) and the *trobar ric* (a poem deliberately ornate and verbally intricate). See *In Praise*, pp. 120-30.

In translating this poem, I have used the format from Manuscript "Ld," Laurenziana 46-60 folio 32 verso, taken from Pound's *Cavalcanti*, pp. 170-76. The staggered verses suggest the modern technique of open or field composition, something that lends itself very well to such an expansive poem.

J. E. Shaw provides an extended prose translation of this poem along with a literal commentary in his *Guido Cavalcanti's Theory of Love* (Toronto: University of Toronto Press, 1949).

Poem 28
In this comic sonnet, Cavalcanti parodies his constant use of the term "spirit."

Poem 29
This poem and the next treat Cavalcanti's experience on a pilgrimage to Santiago de Compostela. During this trip, Corso Donati tried to have our poet murdered.

Poem 30
This *ballata media* has a *stanza* with two *piedi* of AB and a *ripresa* and *sirima* of Bcccx.

The public aspect of love in this ballad calls to mind chapters 3-5 in Dante's *La Vita Nuova* where Dante comes upon Beatrice in the company of others.

Line 13: as in chapter 3 of Dante's *La Vita Nuova*, where Beatrice initiates her message with her eyes, Cavalcanti's deeper communication with his maidens begins when they turn their eyes toward him.

Line 41: again, the ultimate communication occurs with the eyes.

Line 46: *La Dorata* is the church of Notre-Dame de la Daurade in Tolosa, Spain.

Poem 31

This *ballata mezzana* consists of a *stanza* with two *piedi* of AB, a *sirima* of BXX, and a *ripresa* of Y(y)XX.

Cavalcanti develops the idea of the eyes as a force to be reckoned with. The imagery connected with vision is intense: *occhi* (eyes); *sguardo* (I look); *occhi suoi* (her eyes); *veggio* (I see); *Ella si vede* (literally, "She sees herself," but the sense is "She seems"); *ch'om...l'aridsca mirare* (any man...daring to look at her); and *s'i' la sguardasse* (if I would look).

Poem 32

In this *ballata mezzana,* the *ripresa* consists of XyyX, *stanze* of AbC, AbC, and a *sirima* of CddX.

Cavalcanti deals with the double-edged theme of the pain and joy of love; e.g., drawing life from death.

Line 3: *di tanta noia* ("so much trouble") anticipates Dante's *Inferno* (I, 76) where Virgil asks him, "Ma tu, perché ritorni a tanta noia?" ("But why did you return to such trouble?"). In both cases, joy and suffering are linked. For example, in this passage from the *Inferno, noia* rhymes with *gioia.* Further, Dante is happy to see Virgil whose *bello stile* in his epic, *The Aeneid,* made him call Virgil his master, his author. Yet, his pleasure and knowledge do not come without the arduous labor symbolized by the slowly ascending journey he is undertaking. As we have seen, at times Cavalcanti draws pleasure from suffering, too. See note to Poem 15 for further discussion of this paradox.

Poem 33

Guinizelli uses the term *disaventura* (Contini, 2:473) in lamenting that a young lady did not return his love.

Poem 34

This *ballata mezzana* has a *stanza* with two *piedi* of AB AB and a *sirima* and *ripresa* of BcC.

Line 25-26: Dante (Dante Alighieri, *Rime*, ed. Contini, pp. 107-9) begins one of his sonnets with the verse, "Parole mie che per lo mondo siete" ("My words who are out in the world"), invoking poetry's traditional power to instruct and delight.

Poem 35

This *ballata mezzana* consists of a *stanza* of two *piedi* of AB AB and a *sirima* and *ripresa* of Bccddx. Cavalcanti probably wrote this ballad while suffering political exile in Sarzana.

Line 10: *che sia nemica di gentil natura* (literally, "those who are enemies of gentle nature") is a passage that reveals the wide range of material – here, politics – allegorized with love poetry. To be of a "gentle nature" one must know the rules of Love. In this sense, the knowledge shared by refined and noble lovers leads to harmony. Dissonance occurs when base people are ignorant of the rules. This pattern parallels the world of politics. When the same knowledge or political opinion is shared, harmony results. When people do not have the same knowledge or opinion, their ignorance makes them dissonant.

Line 37: in reference to Cavalcanti's "terrified and weakened voice," remember that he caught malaria at Sarzana and was to die shortly. When he speaks of death "squeezing me" (Line 18), he must have known at this time that his usual figurative death was more than poetic drama.

Poem 36

In two Renaissance manuscripts, this poem is next to Dante's sonnets of correspondence. Because of this and also the subject matter, it is considered a missive to Dante (Contini, 2:543).

Line 2: literally, "Of the grave state my heart bears." *Porta* in this sense means "bear" as in carrying a burden. Cino da Pistoia uses *porta* in the same sense in his sonnet "O lasso! ch'io credea trovar pietate." See *Rimatori del dolce stil novo,* ed. Luigi di Benedetto (Turin: UTET, 1925), p. 132.

Line 7: *[i]ngiuliosa* is semiliterary duecento Tuscan for *ingiurioso* (injurious or unjust).

Poems 37A and 37B

"A ciascun'alma presa" is the first poem in Dante's *La Vita Nuova.* Cavalcanti's response is one his most famous poems.

Poem 37B, Line 1: *Vedeste, al mio parere...* literally means "You would see, according to me...."

Line 6: *casser* is an apocopated (shortened) version of *cassero,* the citadel of a castle.

Poem 38A

Dante's sonnet to Guido that treats love as a voyage of magical enchantment, harkening back to the legend of King Arthur.

Line 1: Lapo Gianni was a notary and a *stilnovisto* poet.

Line 2: *incantamento* can denote both enchantment as a magical spell and allurement as an amorous charm. Both are applicable to the effects of love.

Line 3: Contini (Dante, *Rime*, p. 35) identifies *vasel* as the ship of Merlin.

Line 9: *monna Vanna* was Guido's lady and *monna Lagia* was Lapo's.

Line 10: *de le trenta* refers to the list of thirty beautiful ladies that was kept in Florence. Since we know that Beatrice was number 9 on the list, we can assume that number 30 was one of the two "screen" ladies from *La Vita Nuova*.

Line 12: *ragionar* literally means "to reason" or "to think." It implies mental activity to discover knowledge or "to inquire." It can also mean "to discuss."

Poem 38B

This sonnet is Cavalcanti's response to Dante's "Guido i' vorrei."

Poem 39

In this sonnet, Cavalcanti asks Dante about Lapo Gianni, another of the *stilnovisti*. Notice in the *terzine* that *vile* does not rhyme with *sire*. Contini (2:547) points out that Favati's attempt with Codex Mezzabarba's version of *uomo non può che sia vile servire* is weak. Nelson (p. 115) settles on *om che sia vile non vi può servire*. There is the possibility, especially given Cavalcanti's ability to transcend any tedious habit of thought, that he did not intend perfect rhyme, but settled on assonance.

Poem 40

This sonnet refers to Dante's call at the beginning of *La Vita Nuova* for dreams of Love.

Lines 5-6: *'l servitore di monna Laggia* refers to Lapo Gianni by way of his lady, Mistress Laggia.

Line 13: Another possibility is "kept to do his [Love's] pleasure."

Poem 41

Cavalcanti addresses Dante in this sonnet. Contini (2:548) contends that the Dante's "vile thoughts" are the result of Beatrice's death. On the other hand, Ciccuto (p. 146) thinks that Guido is criticizing the period of Dante's poetry that treated love more lightly.

Poem 42

Cavalcanti rebukes a friend for having broken off a relationship with a young lady.

Line 6: *...da quella ch'è nel tondo sesto* (literally, "from that [girl] who is in the sixth circle"). Contini (2:550) suggests that this "sixth circle" may refer to the sixth *sesto*, one of Florence's administrative divisions; and/or the sixth planet of Giove, referring to a lady named Giovanna.

Poem 43

This *mottetto* is Cavalcanti's reply to Gianni Alfani's sonnet "Guido, quel Gianni." Although rhymed in couplets *(rime bacciate),* the verse length is irregular throughout.

Line 1: refers to Andreas Capellanus' treatise on love, *De Amore.*

Line 12: *e·cco'* is a dialectical contraction of *e* and *con* ("and with"). See note to Poem 9 for further explanation.

Lines 14-15: literally, "Because God's Church/will want a fief for justice."

Poems 44A and 44B

Bernardo da Bologna and Cavalcanti spar in these courtly jibes.

Poem 44A, line 5: *Udistù* is *udisti tu* ("have you heard") with the pronoun in an enclitic position.

Poem 44B, lines 3-4: Nelson (p. 71) translates *...solo da quella/ che ti rispuose a le tue rime agute* as "from her alone/Who replied to your shrewd rimes." However, *solo da* can also mean "except for" or "aside from," which conveys Cavalcanti's nastiness more effectively.

Poem 45

Contini (2:554) suggests that Cavalcanti is addressing a friend who has taken a house in the country. The *santalena* was an antique coin named for Saint Helen, Constantine's mother, which was perhaps worn as a pendant. Could the sardonic mood of this sonnet indicate that this little jewel was indeed another woman?

Poem 46

The *ballata minore* uses a *stanza* of two AB *piedi* and a *ripresa* and *sirima* of B(b)X. It is in the tradition of the pastoral (a genre

151

exploited well by the Provençal troubadours), a poem in which a young noble encounters and woos a shepherdess.

Poem 47

Cavalcanti mocks Fra Guittone d'Arezzo's scholastic reasonings about love, in particular his *Trattato d'Amore,* a sequence of thirteen poems with some prose about the evils of worldly love. See *Le rime di Guittone d'Arezzo,* ed. Francesco Egidi, Bari: Laterza, 1940, pp. 268-77.

Line 2: a syllogism is a three-part form of logical reasoning that we today call a major premise, minor premise, and a conclusion. Cavalcanti calls our conclusion the minor premise. Between it and the major premise is a middle premise.

Poems 48A-50B

This *tenzone* between Cavalcanti and Guido Orlandi, a minor contemporary of Cavalcanti known for his attempts at literary sparring, focuses on two issues (Contini, 2:558-65). First, Cavalcanti refers to the painting of the Virgin at Florence's church of Orto San Michele that allegedly began weeping on July 3, 1292. The miracle was subsequently discredited by both the Dominicans and Franciscans. The last *terzina* of Poem 48A provides us with Cavalcanti's penetrating appraisal of the politics of miracles.

Second, the underlying question here is the issue of who is the real poet. Although Poems 49A and 50A deal with the subject of celestial versus worldly love, that is mere pretense for Cavalcanti cajoling Orlandi as a Scholastic hack.

Both Cavalcanti and Orlandi conclude their respective debate using the verb *limare,* which means "to polish," but which has a root noun *limo* that can mean either "body" or "mud." It is a testimony to Orlandi's lack of subtlety that he resorts to such an obvious pun. Cavalcanti, on the other hand, in the penetrating manner of the *stil nuovo,* goes to the heart of Orlandi's weaknesses. Our poet uses the traditional love imagery of archery to point out Orlandi's inability to do anything beyond the ordinary and tried-and-true. Further, Cavalcanti attacks Orlandi's aesthetic as originating from the unimaginatively obvious (50A, line 12: "...something you can hold in your hand").

Poem 48B, line 2: *gratïa plena et pia* is Latin for "full of grace and pure.

Line 5: *Et veritas et via* is Latin for "the Truth and the Way."

Poem 49A, lines 4 and 10: *co·llei* is dialect for *con lei* ("with her"); *i·llei* is dialect for *in lei* ("in her"). See note to Poem 9 for further explanation.

Poem 49B, line 5: *Gioiosa Garda* (literally, "Joyous Guard") is referring to the knights of the Round Table from Arthurian legend.

Poem 50A: a *sonetto caudato* with a *disticco* added to a regular sonnet.

Poem 51

This poem, replete with Florentine dialect, is one of Cavalcanti's "burlesque" sonnets. Its source is the Italian *beffa*, a particularly cruel, mocking type of joke. For example, Don Rodrigo's prank against Renzo and Lucia in *I promessi sposi* is in this vein. Cavalcanti's pre-Enlightenment mockery of the hunchback calls to mind Verdi's character Rigoletto, without any of Verdi's humanity and sympathy. See also the extended *beffa* in Antonio Manetti, *The Fat Woodworker,* trans. and ed. Robert L. Martone and Valerie Martone (New York: Italica Press, 1991).

In the first quatrain the *-uzza* ending is pejorative. In the second it is a diminutive endearment. See Rohlfs, 3:371-72.

Poem 52

In this sonnet, Cavalcanti engages in sharp invective against one of his kin, Nerone Cavalcanti. In June 1304, four years after our poet's death, Nerone led the disturbances in Florence that led to burning the houses of the Cavalcanti and their expulsion from the city (Contini, 2:567). The mocking tone tells us that Guido did not think much of Nerone's prowess or integrity.

Line 14: *sì fosti paziente del mercato* translates literally as "if you were patient in the marketplace"; i.e., "if you could tolerate the transaction" – in this case, perhaps a reference to Nerone's inability to make the proper moral choice between his political independence and his financial security.

INDEX OF FIRST LINES

This Book Was Completed on May 1, 1992 at
Italica Press, New York, New York and was
Set in Garamond. It Was Printed on 50 lb
Glatfelter Natural, Acid-Free Paper
With a Smyth-Sewn Binding by
McNaughton & Gunn
Ann Arbor, MI
U. S. A.
* *
*